# No Small Feat!

# No Small Feat!

## Taking Time for Change

Pearl Gold Solomon

CORWIN PRESS, INC.
A Sage Publications Company
Thousand Oaks, California

Copyright © 1995 by Corwin Press, Inc.

All rights reserved. No part of this book may be reproduced or utilized in any form or by any means, electronic or mechanical, including photocopying, recording, or by any information storage and retrieval system, without permission in writing from the publisher.

*For information address*:

Corwin Press, Inc.
A Sage Publications Company
2455 Teller Road
Thousand Oaks, California 91320

SAGE Publications Ltd.
6 Bonhill Street
London EC2A 4PU
United Kingdom

SAGE Publications India Pvt. Ltd.
M-32 Market
Greater Kailash I
New Delhi 110 048 India

Printed in the United States of America

**Library of Congress Cataloging-in-Publication Data**

Solomon, Pearl G. (Pearl Gold), 1929-
   No small feat! Taking time for change / Pearl G. Solomon.
     p.   cm.
   Includes bibliographical references and index.
   ISBN 0-8039-6281-9 (c: alk. paper).—ISBN 0-8039-6282-7 (p: alk. paper)
     1. Education—United States.  2. Classroom environment—United States.  3. Educational change—United States.  I. Title.
LA217.2.S65  1995
370'.973—dc20                                                             95-14404

This book is printed on acid-free paper.

95  96  97  98  99  10  9  8  7  6  5  4  3  2  1

Corwin Press Production Editor: Gillian Dickens
Corwin Press Typesetter: Andrea D. Swanson

# Contents

| | |
|---|---|
| Foreword by Seymour B. Sarason | vii |
| Preface | ix |
| About the Author | xiii |
| 1. Drawing the Map for Change | 1 |
| 2. Understanding the Roles of Visions and Voices | 17 |
| 3. Knowing the Setting and Its History | 33 |
| 4. Leadership: The Judicious Management of Power | 57 |
| 5. Evoking Change With Support and Pressure | 77 |
| 6. Changing People: The Power of New Capacity | 105 |
| 7. Making It Your Own: Assimilation and Reculturization | 135 |
| 8. The Fourth Dimension: Time | 161 |
| Epilogue | 181 |
| References | 183 |
| Index | 189 |

# Foreword

About attempts to change schools there is description, and there is description. By this, I mean that most descriptions leave the readers puzzled about what happened and why. When we finish reading most of these descriptions, we are not clear about what we learned and what the author wanted us to learn. We certainly do not (or certainly rarely) feel that we have received a set of principles well illustrated by cogent, compelling narrative so that we are not at sea about what we should think and do to spearhead a school change effort. Giving readers a set of principles is not all that difficult, but it is, in my experience, a waste of time if those principles are not embedded in clear, compelling, concrete examples of what is meant by planning, process, patience, frustration tolerance, and the inevitably messy context of decision making. School change is not for the fainthearted; neither is it for those unable or unwilling to proceed except to their own drumbeats. Nor is it for those who think that systemic change can occur and improve educational performance without changing what goes on in the classroom. You can change systems, but if you have not changed the classroom, you have been shadowboxing.

Dr. Solomon has written an uncommonly practical book about the complexity of school change. She has not pandered to the readers, talked down to them, or resorted to sermonizing. She has written in a refreshingly clear, thought-provoking style that reveals a humble but strong person. Few teachers or administrators will finish this book without saying, "She understands us, she knows what we think and feel, and she does not make it easy. But at the same time, she causes us to start to think, to see school change not only as *school* change but *personal* change as well." That is no small feat!

Seymour B. Sarason
*Yale University*

# Preface

At one point in the story ahead, a comment reminds readers that it is easy to complain about what is wrong but that it requires energy and time to take the steps to make things right. Perhaps it is time to stop complaining about the difficulty of the complex task of changing schools and to begin again to take the necessary steps. I believe that readers of this book will be able to engage in the process of evolving the collegial cultures that nurture improved practice with a greater chance of success and survival.

What should help readers become the *fittest* is an organization of ideas that takes them one step at a time over the hurdles of the process of change as it maps the paths, identifies the hazards that are known, alerts them to the unknowns, and promises the rewards. Embedded within this organization, however, is a particular story of transformation in which I played a role. It is a story that offers hope for schools and for the people who live, work, and learn in them; it is also one that makes some practical suggestions and provides "how to do it" lists for those who prefer not to depend on chance (although as readers shall see, serendipity helps).

Like any good story, it has real heroes and heroines. They are Elaine, Lila, Sandy, Deanna, Tom, and Alan, the teachers; and Meg and Anne, the principals. All were evocators or leaders of change, and I believe they will be an inspiration to a whole new generation of teacher-leaders, like the ones sitting in my own classes. There are also some villains, but they are not really bad. They are just examples of people trying to do their best in their own way and who are therefore resistant to the intrusions of others. Because this is a real story, not a fairy tale, there are highs and lows along the way, and not everything comes out just right.

To be more specific, this is a book about restructuring and reculturization, about changing curriculum, and about reforming school governance; it is also a story about what makes schools work. It includes episodes that describe the nature of current efforts and needs for school reform (Chapter 1); the visions and voices that must be considered (Chapter 2); the history and setting that require attention but that can become important connections (Chapter 3); the giving and using of power by different sources of leadership—especially teacher-leaders (Chapter 4); the way these leaders use pressure and support to get change going (Chapter 5); the many ways in which new capacity can be constructed and its ultimate dependence on each individual's reflections in action (Chapter 6); and the importance of consensual contracts for curriculum and assessment, which are needed for reculturization and the maintenance of change (Chapter 7). Last, Chapter 8 illustrates (perhaps for the first time) how time in its three perspectives—as a resource, in its passage, and in the sense of timeliness (which may only be chance or serendipity)—is a variable of great importance.

Although recent episodes that relate how the mathematics curriculum was transformed within the context of a change in governance are emphasized, I have included other examples from my extensive background as an educator and from the experiences of others. Because many of the ideas on the process of change are not original (although there may be some new ones), I have shared the thoughts of those others who are presently, or have been in the past, engaged in understanding how change happens.

For all the preceding reasons, this book may be useful for anyone who has a present or future leadership role in the process of improving schools. It is appropriate for the general reading interests of teachers, administrators, and educational policymakers and can serve as a manual for those who need some specific guidance. The book can also work well as a basic text for courses in curriculum and leadership.

Readers may also be interested in knowing what this book is not about. It is certainly not the book it started out to be: a program evaluation report to a new superintendent of schools. It began merely as a chronology, supported by some convincing quantitative data. But in trying to add some of the context and detail, I realized that there was quite a story to tell—a story worth sharing with others.

In writing the first version for other readers, I believed that they needed to know about the current research in cognitive science, which (along with some of our own findings) helped my colleagues and me to come to new understandings about how learning takes place and how mathematical ideas are constructed. It also seemed important to include my statistical methods, data, and analyses. Reviewers, however, seemed much more interested in the transformations that I described. This version, therefore, has eliminated most of the specifics of the mathematics and quantitative data. Instead, I have added many ideas and details on the process of change and related these to the current literature on school reform.

Specifics are important because for change to be accepted, it must have meaning and real purpose for those who are to be affected by it. Perhaps the math will be a different book; meanwhile, my notes and citations may help direct readers to other sources. The data analyses may no longer be fresh enough for publication, but I would be happy to share them and my instrumentations with any reader-researcher who is interested. The curriculum and assessments described in Chapter 7 are also available.

Many people have helped along the way. I specifically thank Ann Lieberman of Teachers College, who gave me my first encouragement to proceed; Walter Secada, an early reviewer who set me straight on some misconceptions but was impressed enough to include me in his working group on school reform at the University of Wisconsin; Brian Ellerbeck, an editor at Teachers College Press who helped me get rid of my "researchspeak"; Alice Foster, my editor at Corwin Press, who finally set me straight about priorities and offered so many helpful suggestions; Seymour Sarason, who inspired and guided my previous endeavors with his writings, provided this book with many ideas that I hope I have confirmed, and graciously offered to review it; my husband, Mel, and my colleague and friend Sister Teresa O'Connor at St. Thomas Aquinas College, both of whom were constant supports through this long process; and last but not least, the many teachers and principals from whom I have learned so much.

# About the Author

**Pearl Gold Solomon** is an Associate Professor of Teacher Education at St. Thomas Aquinas College in Sparkill, New York, where she teaches graduate courses in curriculum and teaching. Although a newcomer to the academic environment, she has spent many years in education as a change agent in public schools. Her roles in K-12 schools included those of teacher, counselor, and administrator at both the building and central office levels.

She has an EdD in educational administration from Teachers College, Columbia University, where she first developed her interest in the process of change. Her present interests also include developing teacher-leaders and improving mathematics and science education. Recent research papers have dealt with team teaching and the nature of peer interactions among in-service teachers.

She is the director of the Marie Curie Mathematics and Science Center at St. Thomas Aquinas College. The center, which works with schools and industry to offer programs directly to secondary students and K-12 teachers, has recently been validated by the state of New York for program dissemination purposes.

# 1

# Drawing the Map for Change

## About Schools

Listening to the conversations of parents as they wait for their children at the end of the school day or during soccer practice has been an illuminating piece of research for this incognito educator in her grandmother role. Most of their comments about the school and the educational process have had little to do with the changing needs of society or its technological future. The parents seemed unimpressed with new curriculum and classroom computers but very concentrated on the present nature of that individual and traditional relationship of their children with the classroom teachers. It was easy to sense a certain level of anxiety about the power that teachers have over the lives of their children.

Despite this anxiety, schools may represent a comforting safety net for parents concerned about the unpredictable and rapidly changing world around them. Through time, people tend to remember the pleasant things the most. We connect schools with the security of our own childhoods and like the idea of continuity. It is all right to dabble with things that are new, but at least one foot needs to be firmly planted in a tried and proved system: a system that had its origins in the time schedules, calendars, and one-room independent schools of this country's agrarian history. This system changed little when these units were placed side by side in the multiclassroom buildings that were predicated by a shift to an industrial society.

The values of independence, individuality, and competition that single-classroom, single-teacher units nurture represent the historical ethos of the American culture. Such values have made innovations such as cooperative learning[1] more acceptable to teachers than to parents who want their own children to learn to compete—not as a group, but as individuals. Educators need to pay attention to the values, anxieties, and expectations of parents, but we also need to take the initiative for improvement and do a much better job of communicating new ideas to them. Educators are the professionals who should know better! It is most unfortunate when an uninformed community is aligned with internal school system forces, both human and organizational, that are positioned to maintain the present order and resist change. This makes schools, as Sarason (1990, 1993) has noted, intractable and unresponsive to the needs of a changing world.

Even in an era in which the culture is framed and altered on a daily basis by a common and universally affecting media, when human interaction and the transfer of knowledge is facilitated by the technology of a vast information highway, schools cling to the old habits of comforting boundaries in their settings. Lortie (1975) described teachers as *bounded* in their classrooms, resentful of any interruption from administrator, parent, school function, or colleague who interferes with their closed-door opportunity to "reach" their students. Schools and their leaders have often been similarly bounded from their surrounding social systems and from other schools. They sometimes have tunnel vision, which eschews what has temporality and is successful in other places. The problem with this is that the resulting isolation provides neither the optimum environment for the construction of new knowledge nor the visions for change. It is people's ability to communicate with each other that creates our cognitive strength and sets the human species apart.

Changing schools requires ongoing communication within and without the system and sometimes an upheaval of the patterns that satisfy human needs. Upheavals are always discomfiting, but reflecting and sharing the pain with one's peers can be helpful. Interaction between peers can also help with the construction of new knowledge and the solutions to problems. Recent attempts to restructure schools have recognized the value of interaction. They have tried to dissolve

# Drawing the Map for Change

some boundaries by encouraging shared decision making among teachers, administrators, and parents as they work together to improve the quality of education. The following anecdote introduces these new attempts and offers an example of the potential benefits of improved interactions between the leaders of schools. More will follow.

## A Glimpse of the Present

For a while, it seemed like déjà vu. Here I was, in the spring of 1994, attending a meeting of countywide assistant superintendents and curriculum directors. The present faces were not unfamiliar to me. They were those of my former colleagues from South Vale[2] and others with whom I was presently engaged in a cooperative venture. As the discussion began, I recalled my first such meetings with their counterparts 23 years ago.

It had been a disheartening shock to see the previous group in action. Their stated purpose of communication and shared problem solving seemed to be subsumed by a driving need for each individual in turn to strut his or her stuff—while ignoring or sarcastically cutting down what anybody else was saying or doing. They were the manifestation, at the leadership level, of the isolation and preserves of power that existed in education at the time and often still exist. Competition, not consensus, was their agenda.

There was palpable tension in this new group of the present, but I soon realized that it had to do with their frustration over the agenda. And although they were still interrupting each other, it was mostly for productive interaction. Everyone was listening with interest to how others would deal with the current crisis, and all showed real passion for what they were doing. They had actually invited me (a new academic who had come from their ranks) to attend as a consultant, hoping that I could provide some help.

The problem that had created such anxiety and was the main purpose of this session concerned two recent mandates from the New York State Education Department. Following the issuance of *The New Compact for Learning* (University of the State of New York, 1991), the commissioner of education had issued two separate regulations for implementation by local school districts. All of the districts were in the process of planning for compliance or actually implementing these regulations. One of the mandates required the districts to initiate site-based management teams, a restructuring of school governance that calls for participation by teachers and parents. This mandate also specified other parameters such as the creation of conflict resolution committees in case the predictable differences got in the way. The second separate mandate called for the development of local benchmarks and standards for student achievement. Confusion about the meaning and limits of these terms reigned.

A complication related to the implementation of these mandates was the unbelievable political response to a flourishing new item on the educational menu: a focus on outcomes. Nationally based conservative groups had objected to the idea of everyone being held accountable to the same outcome. Concerned that this fallout might enjoin their new mandates, the New York State Education Department had issued a whole new set of definitions for the preferred term of *standard*. In previous documents issued as late as the fall of 1993, *outcome* or *outcome standard* were commonly used terms.

In my own definition bank, an outcome was the same thing as a receiver-based goal or behavioral objective (educators have been safely using these for years); for example, "the student will be able to communicate effectively," or, more specifically, "the student will know how a topic sentence frames a paragraph." An objective (or outcome) with a measurable standard attached to it would be a performance-based objective. The outcome could also be based on the performance of a school. One curriculum director said that the standards would be stated as outcomes for schools as measured by improved performance on a standardized test. Whatever the terminology, the purpose of the state mandate was for each district to clarify and document what it expected to accomplish for its students.

Unfortunately, most of the districts, anxious to comply and be current, had already begun to develop some teacher ownership in the concept of outcome-based education. Participants at this county-wide meeting discussed this for a while, and I showed them how the disfavored terms could be interchanged with the recommended ones without loss of meaning. But those who had already begun to use the outcome terminology said they would stick to it. I didn't blame them a bit. Transferring ownership of a new concept is not an easy task. On the surface, schools seem vulnerable to the undulating pressures of public interests. They usually try to respond, but underneath the surface, a rigidity makes response difficult, and this rigidity only strengthens with repeated and contradictory attempts to intrude.

# Drawing the Map for Change

Strangely, although the state education department was specific about terms and other minutiae, it had not in any way connected these two mandates. Therefore, another big question for this meeting was "How are your mandated implementation activities related?" I presumed that they certainly would be. After all, shouldn't site-based teams have something to say about district standards? Surprise! Only two of the six districts represented actually had the site-based teams select the committees to develop standards. Steve, a recently appointed assistant superintendent, gave a convincing and emotional rationale for deciding to separate the tasks.

Steve had been part of the faculty for two successive summer institutes that I had organized for teachers from several of the districts. An expert on peer coaching, he understood how to gain the teachers' trust and how to get them to trust each other. It was obvious from Steve's passion that he had been intensely involved in a strong effort in his district to implement both mandates, but he told us that in contrast to other districts, his district purposely started with the standards rather than with the site-based management. "We wanted to put a lens on the outcomes and standards because that is what is important! We felt that if we started with site-based teams, energy and attention would be diverted to other issues. And we only have teachers on the standards teams, because they are the professionals," he explained.

"We could never get away with that—we would have parents down our backs!" was the response of another assistant superintendent. "We asked the site-based teams to choose members of the standards committee," commented a director of elementary education. "Our principals are our major problem—they want veto power," said another.

My biggest surprise came from my former colleagues. Jim was the assistant superintendent and Nate was the curriculum director from South Vale, my former district. Unlike the other districts, South Vale had a long history of site-based management. They were now in their 7th year of team operation, with parent involvement for the last 3 years. Nate broke the unexpected news. "The executive board of the teachers union wanted to appoint the standards committee, but we wouldn't consider it. Our standards committee is separate from the site-based teams. The site-based teams are not doing very much anymore." As an afterthought, he said, "but maybe they should validate what the standards committee does." A chill of disappointment was my first reaction. Why had such a hopeful reform deteriorated?

My spirits were somewhat lifted when I looked at the materials Jim shared with the group. South Vale had just received a special recognition. It was the only school district in the state to receive an organizational quality award. Their site-based management teams had played a large part in creating and documenting that quality. Separate groups were making progress with the development of standards. A graph of the district's recent performance on an international math test showed spectacular results; it seemed as though my own effort as curriculum director and follow-up as a consultant had met an external standard. Would the internal achievements be sustained? What I heard at the meeting and from other sources raised some doubts.

## The Purpose of This Book

Reflecting on this meeting, I realized that the conclusions I had reached after a quarter century of involvement in the school change process were confirmed. Changing schools is a complex process that takes time and involves many interacting human variables. Because the need for time has been ignored and human variables are difficult to predict, transformation attempts with lofty goals have frequently met a quiet or disruptive demise. In a disheartening report, Mirel (1994) tells the tale of a well-funded and well-meaning major reform effort that fizzled in just a year. He cautions that educational change will not succeed unless reformers pay attention to its material and political dimensions beforehand, and he wonders whether the districts he worked with tried to do too much. I add that they tried to do too much in too little time.

Sarason (1990, 1993) and Fullan (1982) also characterize educational change as a complex and difficult-to-predict process. Fullan suggests, however, that "our cognitive ability to conceptualize, understand, and plan for the social processes of educational change represent the most comprehensive and generative resource for dealing with change" (p. 93). The purpose of this book is to help others construct their own cognitions of these processes through sharing some of what I have learned through time. In the chapters ahead, descriptions of how some predictable variables may affect the outcomes of efforts to transform schools will be accompanied by suggestions for the steps that may control them and increase the probability of success. There are no suggestions for the unpredictable ones, except that it is wise to expect and prepare for them.

Perhaps knowing the predictable variables and expecting the unforeseen eventualities can help propel reformers through the perils of change to a more satisfactory end. For example, readers may discover the undeniable benefits of site-based autonomy. They also may become aware, however, that the existing rewards for the expenditure of energy and time that autonomy demands of teachers may not be sufficient to sustain their effort—especially when they do not have the necessary capacity and when traditional holders of power resist relinquishing some of it. Readers will be encouraged by the finding that although there is not yet any evidence that changes in governance alone will improve outcomes for students, drawing clearer maps for the connections between educational or program reform and the restructuring of school governance offers promise.

Leadership from many sources, including teachers themselves, can help us make the maps, take the steps, and monitor our progress. The nature of that leadership is another variable worth understanding. It may be useful to know how power can be used or given by leadership to provide the many forms of support and pressure that are needed for the growth of capacity. Finally, readers will be alerted to the need for patience and vigilance as change makes its required unhurried passage through time.

More specifically, this book will address such questions as these: Will site-based management be the panacea and solve our educational problems? Will an increase in teachers' autonomy make them more receptive to new forms of practice? How can site-based teams avoid burnout, and how do we deal with the career patterns that through time diminish individual motivations to change? Can we productively connect program changes and school-based autonomy? Meanwhile, can effective collegiality exist in many different forms? Can teachers work with parents on site-based teams and work simultaneously in different groups or clusters with evocators of change on standards or curriculum committees? Can we revise the traditional patterns of roles and power sources and use the power of teacher-leaders to evoke change? How can we deal with the limits of capacity and time? Can we overcome the vicissitudes of political winds and the governmental pressures they inspire? Can we ever succeed in attempts to improve schools and make them more internally responsive to the evolving world?

I think we have been successful at some times and in some places. Knowing the patterns for these successes and understanding how the variables of change enmesh the people, fashion the events, and determine the outcomes of our transformation efforts may tip the balance away from failure. The important thing to remember, however, is that this effort never ends. If schools are not involved in changing for the better, they are in the process of decay. They never stay the same.

## Connecting School and Program Reform

Most efforts to transform schools in the past have been more narrowly directed at specific programs, instructional strategies, or organization. Only recently have efforts been aimed toward systemic change, especially changes that affect the governance of schools. Unfortunately, as it usually occurs, the direction suggested for this change in governance is conflicting. At the same time that recommendations are made to increase the local involvement of parents and teachers, there are calls for national standards. When people or institutions are pulled in two different directions, we are inclined to resist and safely stand still. This may not be a wise solution. Instead, we may need to take a better look at our internal mechanisms and decide which of these external pressures to change fit. We may conclude that neither of them do or that only parts of each will help, but the introspection will be useful.

This type of introspection began for me as I reflected on a specific educational program change in which the teaching of elementary mathematics had been essentially restructured, and minor, but important, revisions had been made at the secondary level. I recalled the conflicts, anxieties, pain, revelations, and minor and major failures and triumphs of this recent episode and connected them to my previous knowledge gathered through lengthy experience as an educator involved almost constantly in serious attempts to improve schools. I realized that the effort to change curriculum, which took place in the context of a systemic change in governance, provided a framework for understanding the many, but more often separate, efforts to reform the schools of the 1990s.

At first, I didn't make the connection between the program change and a major concurrent endeavor to improve the schools via site-based shared decision making. My vision for what I had wanted to happen in mathematics was clear, as was my commitment to the need for teacher involvement in any change process. It certainly seemed, at the beginning, that the district-wide focus on management reform was draining energy and attention from the separate efforts to change curriculum and instruction. The confusion about who was going to make specific decisions also encumbered the implementation of the new mathematics program, especially when it came time to move it beyond the original pilot and decision-making group of teachers to every classroom. "I thought we were having shared decision making. I didn't vote on this new math program," was the comment at a faculty meeting.

Not until I began to compare the circumstances and progress of the two efforts for reform did the patterns that explained similarities or differences and the interactive effects become clear. The strength and nature of these patterns and effects may be determined by the many variables that compose the individual context of change, but any attempt to empower teachers by restructuring the management of schools would have little impact on students unless it was coupled with concurrent efforts to empower teachers with a new perspective and better skills in their craft. The opposite case is also true: To be effective, teachers need greater autonomy over the situations in which they practice their craft—not necessarily complete individual control, but a collegial voice.

Fullan, Bennett, and Bennett (1990) support this conclusion when they state that teachers must develop the generic capacity to master "an array of instructional models" and conduct "constant inquiry" (p. 17). But they further state that recent research suggests that (a) single program changes alone cannot make a major difference, (b) classroom and total school improvement must be linked, and (c) teachers should be "collaborative as a way of working" (p. 17).

On the basis of his knowledge of the complex and intractable nature of schools and the traditional and bureaucratic power relationships within them, Sarason (1990) predicted the failure of reform that hinges on a change only in school management. He suggested (1993) that the only possibility for true reform is to change the preparation of teachers. His predictions are affirmed by recent studies of efforts to move toward site-based shared decision making, including large-scale reforms in Rochester, New York, and Dade County, Florida, in which the change in school management has not shown an increase in student achievement (e.g., Berger, 1991; Weiss, 1993).

These studies, however, found that the overall climate for teachers and students is improved by shared decision making. My discoveries concur with this. The difference in the South Vale experience was that we did not rely on management changes alone to improve the schools. As those previously cited have suggested, we also helped the teachers construct new capacity in their craft, and we did not depend on one-shot, time-limited skill development workshops to do this. Sarason (1990) also cautions that it is difficult to determine a starting point for change. We decided on simultaneous starting points for change efforts in management and instructional processes, got the instructional improvements we sought, and attribute our success, in part, to the paired efforts. Once we overcame the energy-draining competition for time and resources, the generally improved climate of collaborative and site-based management helped us to implement and institutionalize our specific instructional change. It also staged the opportunity to compare the two changes in terms of the variables that determined their disparate levels of both initial and sustained success.

## Reflective Practice: The Functional Level of Change

Schön (1983, 1987) believes that rather than having a cognitive base on which to make educational decisions, teachers have an *appreciation system,* which is the sum of their theory and practice knowledge and the values that influence their perceptions and definitions. He suggests, further, that the bulk of teachers' learning comes through continuous action and reflection in action or subsequent reflection on action as they try to solve everyday problems. Schön envisions the teacher as a *reflective practitioner* and the teaching process as a complex situation-specific art.

The values of teachers' appreciation systems can be interpreted to include the standards by which they measure themselves and their students; this logically connects reflective practice to the process of assessment. Immediate assessment and appropriate response are parts of the most often isolated, dynamic, and situation-bound classroom experience. When reflections on action are shared with peers, they are a form of assessment that may generate responses that are

# Drawing the Map for Change

not immediate but are of great benefit. Long-term reflective assessments also have a role—not assessments imposed meaninglessly by others but those designed to provide a picture of long-term effectiveness of practice in terms of a true consensus of values. These values or standards should represent all who are involved: the students, the parents, and the community. Most important, they need to be internalized by teachers and become part of their reflective practice.

Changing schools implies changing teachers, and it is within the reflective process that change must occur. The successful actions of change that I have observed in the past were generated by reflective, self-assessing teachers and leaders. In a recent experience that I will describe in chapters ahead, the new energies required by individual teachers for planning and implementing changes in practice were strengthened by reflections shared with peers, power-giving supportive leaders, and purposeful assessments. In the rarer instances when pressure from leaders was necessary, it was mitigated by their support and the encouragement of peers.

In time, innovative methods became comfortable habits, but new teachers had to be engaged. Elaine, whom readers will meet again later, reflected on her interactions with her new colleagues. At the beginning of the year, she wrote this:

> I don't feel comfortable going into their classrooms to watch them—because they're so nervous at the idea of doing that. That's why at the beginning of the mentoring program I gave them "ideas" as to how we could accomplish what we wanted to do. They all like the idea of seeing me teach and then meeting to discuss it.

At the end of the year, she wrote, "Helping my four mentorees will undoubtedly continue. We realize the need to support each other with ideas, having dialogue about problems, showing each other something new to try that has worked. We can't stand alone. It is so obvious!"[3]

When she expressed these feelings, Elaine was an experienced and gifted teacher. She had been involved in collegial practice for several years and was committed to increasing her capacity. Now she was sharing her own power with novices but was also gaining new strength for herself and her peers in the process. In reaching this stage and beyond with her, we marked a number of variables that affected the situation-bound differences between her transformations and those of others.

## The Variables of Change

Many attempts have been made to identify the concepts of change and bring them into the consensual domain—or generate ideas of basic agreement. I feel most comfortable with a set of human and situational variables that have, through time, demonstrated their power to affect the school change process—to others as well as to me.

Spady and Marshall (1990) have defined the variables of vision, capacity, ownership, and support as generic bases of transformation in schools. On the basis of my own and others' experience with change, I have added time, power, leadership, history and setting, and pressure to this list. None of the variables are independent: They all interact, but the variable of time may be an overarching control of each of them.

Although teachers are often internally motivated to change, leadership by administrators or colleagues in the form of pressure and support is related to the growth of new capacity. Together these variables can be viewed as the energy-requiring action path of change. They are the engines that drive the process of change in reflective practice, and they require large investments of human energy. The other variables can then be considered as the controls in the ambient culture that affect the initiation and rate of change.

In following chapters, I will explore in detail how each of these variables affects the restructuring processes and how each may be controlled, citing examples from my own and other cultures. For a preview perspective, I address them briefly below. Figure 1.1 illustrates the relative positions of the variables in the ambient culture and in the action path of reflective practice.

*Vision* (Chapter 2), according to Spady and Marshall (1990), allows educators to use a picture of the future to decide what current actions should be. A present and consistent vision can provide direction for change. Two critical qualifiers to the importance of vision are these: A vision must represent the voices of those for whom the vision is intended (Goodson, 1992), and the nature of the change it proposes must be convincing.

*History* (Chapter 3) and its result, the present *setting*, are often the variables that impede the assumption of ownership, especially when

# Drawing the Map for Change

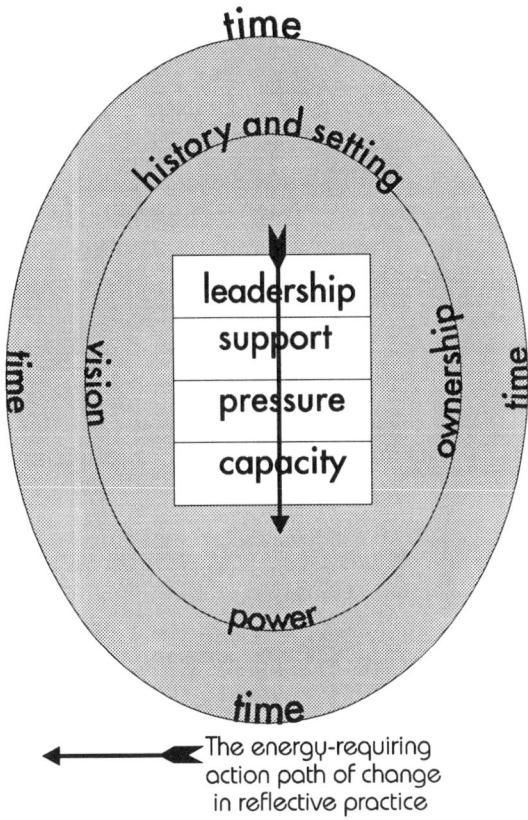

Figure 1.1. The Variables of Change

change disrupts traditional roles. Knowledge of history and making connections to it, however, can be a positive guiding force toward change—a starting place. Connecting new knowledge to previous experience is as effective in the change process as it is in the learning process.

*Leadership* (Chapters 4 and 5) is most often associated with administrative *power*. Good leaders can use their power to control others—but they can also give power to others with their support and by facilitating the growth of capacity. On the other hand, teachers, as leaders in the classroom, value power or control over students. Anything that diminishes their classroom power is viewed with suspicion (Sarason, 1983).

In a collegial culture in which everyone's voice is respected, leadership for change can come from many sources: administrators, outside individuals and groups, and individual teachers and their peer groups. Leadership for change can be multidirectional. For example, reflections by individual teachers or by peer groups can be the source of pressure and support for themselves, but they can also be a source of leadership for change that creates pressure or provides support for administrators. No matter what the source, those who are led need the security that comes from consistency in the direction or vision of leadership.

*Support* by leaders has often been linked with its counterpart, *pressure* (Chapters 5 and 6). Huberman and Miles (1986) combine these in what they refer to as "supported enforcement" or its sustained form, "assistance" (p. 72). Support can come in many forms. Pressure needs the company of support, and it differs from support only in the way power is managed. Administrators, teachers, and collegial leadership teams need power to provide the actions of support and/or pressure as needed. Because the possession of *power*, however, does not guarantee the appropriate actions for productive change, I place this variable outside of the action path. Like the current in electric lines, power has potential, but it must be delivered to the appropriate machine or encounter resistance to do its work. Support and pressure by leaders are the action path or energy-requiring manifestations of power.

Spady and Marshall (1990) describe the building of new *capacity* (Chapters 6 and 7) as the renewal or acquisition of new knowledge, skills, and orientations, which may require giving some things up while retaining and integrating what must be continued. Once capacity is attained and new practices are comfortably assimilated, capacity drives reflective practice. Clarity in the curriculum, consensus on the desired outcomes, and authenticity in assessments help people gain capacity and power: the power that comes with feelings of success and ability to control. Capacity is a significant action path variable in the change process; its growth and maintenance requires time and the energies of teachers and their leaders.

The result of new capacity should be *ownership* (Chapter 7). Ownership of new practices can require the abandonment of old ones, and shifts in ownership create interim loss of comfort. New ownership and comfort for individuals may therefore need new written curriculum and assessments because they provide the documented frames of reference, evidence, and rewards for change. New ownership and comfort for schools or systems may require that these documentations be consensual.

*Time,* as a resource, in its sense of *zeitgeist* or timeliness and as the fourth dimension through which humans must travel as change occurs, is the final and overarching identified variable. Each individual must replace his or her own previous construct with a new one. Disequilibrium may need to come first. It takes time for people to construct and take ownership of their own new knowledge, and they and their environments may change through time. The conclusions in Chapter 8 are discussed in terms of this variable. The organization of my presentation of the variables roughly follows their impact on the time-bound sequence of preparation, implementation, and maintenance of change.

Educational change in the past has been scuttled by weaknesses in all of these variables. Visions of change were rare or limited to minor aberrations: a superficially new curriculum or an adjustment in schedule or organization. Little attention was paid to the variety of voices and history and to the need to develop new capacity for those required to implement these innovations. Ownership was difficult to attach to teachers who had no power or control over what was formally or legally imposed. They overcame pressure by resorting, instead, to more comfortable and familiar informal choices behind closed doors. Leadership support was erratic and inconsistent, limited to materials or the sometimes inflexible and threatening supervision of administrators. *And never was there enough time.*

The hoped-for benefit for the school change process that may be derived from the involvement of teachers in decision making is that mechanisms for bottom-up or teacher-generated change will be formalized and that teachers will have greater opportunities to reap the regenerating rewards of self-actualization. Top-down imposition of pseudo-collaborative wrappings that obscure the true power preserves will do little to change the present systems, but the opportunity for teachers—and perhaps their client parents—to gain some real control over the task of educating children has promise. Teachers must, however, also be willing to accept responsibility for what they and their peers achieve.

The foregoing does not gainsay that every innovative attempt is unique and subject to the different pressures of different cultures and conditions. Although my primary focus for gleaning insights and generalizations about change is a comprehensive, particular, and recent adventure of 7 years, I have included connections to other experiences of my own, as well as to the insights and experiences of others. Readers may also connect to their own previous adventures. My purpose for the exegesis that follows is to share these perceptions so that those who venture into school improvement will have the benefit of being informed of the nature and possible causes of successes and failures. They will, however, have to construct their own new knowledge.

## Notes

1. For definitive work on cooperative learning, see Johnson and Johnson (1989); Johnson, Johnson, and Johnson-Holubec (1987); Sharan et al. (1984); and Slavin (1983).

2. The name of the district, South Vale, and the names of schools and my colleagues in this book are pseudonyms. But the story is about a real place and real people.

3. Quotes from Elaine here and in other chapters are excerpts from her reflections to me, which were written as part of her training as a mentor.

# 2

# Understanding the Roles of Visions and Voices

### About Visions

Most people have a vision of what could be: perhaps not always a precise goal, but a "view of a realistic, credible, attractive future" (Bennis & Nanus, 1985, p. 89). If that vision provides direction for your own life, it can be of great value. If your vision implies common goals and influences the lives of others, it may have even greater value—unless, of course, you neglect to allow the others a voice (Goodson, 1992). Successful transfer of your vision to those who will be affected by it may depend on its nature and your ability to convince others of its worth, but it will also be affected by your willingness to listen and respond to their voices. For this reason, I refer to the person or group who motivates others to change as the *evocator* of change; the evocator calls forth from others and listens.

This chapter will consider the roles of visions and voices in the process of change. It begins with the origins of a systemic vision based on a global vision: the current wave of school reform. The chapter continues with two examples of my visions that were strengthened by the propitious appearance of supporting global ones and then describes how all became a significant part of a single ecological context. I will also explore how the voices of the ambient culture affected the realization of each of the visions and connect this experience, more generally, to the role of visions and voices in the process of implementing change.

## About Voices

Linguistic researcher Charlotte Linde (see Tannen, 1994) has investigated the way people give orders and communicate expectations of others. Giving orders can be either direct or indirect. When the boss says that the place seems dirty today, he or she is implying indirectly that the employee should clean up. If the boss says, "Get this place cleaned up," he or she is giving a direct order. Like the Japanese, who give indirect orders most of the time, educators and those who wish to influence them are most often indirect.

Linde's research also shows that those in power give both indirect and direct messages to influence the actions of others but that they tend to ignore the indirect messages of others. Those not in power must resort to indirect messages, and they listen and are sensitive to indirect messages. Educators in power may be so blinded by their own visions that they neglect to listen to the voices of the indirectly delivered messages of those over whom they have power. One of the most frequent complaints about administrators that I have heard from teachers is that they do not listen to them. Site-based management, if it fulfills its expectations, could provide *a forum in which direct messages of influence are safe and indirect messages are listened to*—a formal place for teachers' voices. Lacking such a forum, it would be wise for leaders to become more sensitive to indirect messages.

## The Origins of the National Vision for School Restructuring

Quite often the source of a vision is obscure. A vision suddenly appears and becomes a local or national institution. In a study of the development of the current wave of reform in school governance, Ogawa (1994) has identified a network of actors in the development of this vision who were actually individuals working for organizations. The current wave, which emerged in the mid-1980s, was

# Understanding the Roles of Visions and Voices

patterned on precursor independent efforts to engage teachers in site-based decision making that began in the early 1970s in a number of places, including some in Florida and California. Many of these early programs are still in operation. The greater organized wave began in 1986 with the impetus of these policy actors or *organizational entrepreneurs* and their organizations, which included the Carnegie Forum on Education and the Economy and the National Governors Association. They were supported in their efforts by teachers' organizations and particularly by Albert Shanker, president of the American Federation of Teachers (AFT).

Ogawa (1994) credits the rapid spread of the concept to workshops that were jointly sponsored by several influential school administrative organizations and the AFT. Although he does not identify the universities as instrumental in getting the movement going, he does say that it was their stamp of approval and documentations in articles that maintained the momentum.

The nature and timeliness of this concept may have also given it that extra push. The concept appealed to the leaders of teachers' organizations because it promised greater autonomy for them. It also appealed to administrators because of its resemblance to the Japanese-inspired organizational quality efforts that were concurrently penetrating American management. Visions for change must be of convincing value to those who pursue them, but they must also convince the others who must change.

Missing from Ogawa's actors or vision developers are the individual people who would be most affected by these changes: the teachers, parents, and students. There was little attempt to listen directly to their voices. Instead, assumptions were made by significant individuals with power that those who did not have it would welcome the dispersal of power suggested by these reforms. Is it possible for an individual educator to manifest a personal vision? I believe that it is, but as readers shall see, the individual will have to listen to other voices and may need some help—from the others and, perhaps, from fate.

## A Personal Vision

In contrast to the vision developed so methodically and quickly by organizational entrepreneurs, sometimes the source of a vision is an individual inner voice that gnaws or festers for a long time until it has an opportunity to emerge. My own vision for improving mathematics education is an example of this.

Studies of cultures such as those of the Kpelle, Vai, and Gola of Liberia and the Dioula and Baoule of the Ivory Coast[1] have demonstrated that many cognitive skills are derived from outside-of-school culture and practices. Like many children of previous generations, I spent my early life on a farm, where everything was observed and measured: the gallons or pails of milk from each cow and the cow's state of pregnancy, the quarts of feed for each chicken coop, the distance between the seeds planted in measured rows and the probability of their germination or rainfall, the bushels of apples from a given tree, the number of apples in a bushel, and how to improve or deter the fermentation process to get better cider. Fields were divided into fractions of acres, always estimated.

Some children are able to connect experiences such as these to what they learn in school. Not everyone does, but teachers can help. The experiences I had made me comfortable with mathematics and science. Few children today have these opportunities, and so as a beginning teacher in an urban school, I tried to simulate my own experiences. My elementary classroom was a combination zoo and greenhouse. Our rabbits ate our first crop, and an elusive escape artist of a garden snake met me daily when I opened my closet door. My city-dweller students were fascinated but unembarrassed as I tried to explain the daylong interlocked positions of two mating box turtles.

Best of all, I had the opportunity to become involved in an innovative developmental mathematics program. We had bead frames, fraction parts, and thinking cards. But the real name of the game was to estimate and to problem solve. I added, "Forget the paper and pencil, let's do it in our heads." What fun we had! My principal worried (we had standardized tests then, too), but I said, "They'll bury the test"—and they did.

I gave it all up to be a high school science teacher just in time to avoid the pain of the post-*Sputnik* new mathematics. My science students, however, soon noticed the enthusiasm of my voice and the glint in my eye when anything quantitative came up. Later, as a middle school principal, there were minutes, sometimes hours, of pure joy when I would take some poor lost and frustrated souls into my office, close the door, pull out my private store of thinking things,

# Understanding the Roles of Visions and Voices

and try to help them make their own sense out of somebody else's problems.

As I reflected on their difficulties, I realized how minimal their cultural experience with numbers and nature was. It was hard enough to put reason into school math when students had a good store of informal problem-solving skills and confidence in them. These kids were deprived. Other than organized sports, even their games did not provide much in the way of quantitative competition. Those games that did had built-in electronics to keep score. Students were not allowed to wander alone and explore: Most of their "free" time was structured or spent passively in front of the television. The girls were at a special disadvantage: The counting games were superseded by Barbie dolls and soap operas; the cakes came from the bakery or mixes. No wonder their Scholastic Aptitude Test (SAT) scores were so low!

How could I resist these inner voices when I was offered the opportunity to be in charge of the school district's mathematics and science program? I couldn't put everyone back on the farm, but I needed to take a shot at finding a better way. At least I had an idea of what could be: not yet a precise goal, but a vision.

## Visions in Context

Visions are pictures of the future that provide goals and direction. Unfortunately, visions are easily faded by individuals' own distractions and by the incursions of others and time. A vision formed apart from the reality of its context always risks the disappointment of a transitory existence. No matter how well the vision is embedded in present reality, however, unpredicted dissonance with the ever changing context of the future can cause it to be quickly obscured. Fortunately, with the passage of time, my preformed vision of improved mathematics education for the students gained structure and sustenance from a number of propitious changes in context.

Consider the global context first. Schools often make the mistake of either isolating themselves from the greater societal ethos or responding impetuously to its ephemeral bubbles and blips. They present a vision that is in conflict with the way most people are thinking or are led by a media anxious for attention. In 1986, when my vision began to take form, the country was at the tail end of a conservative era of economic growth and expansion. "Back to basics" had been the most prominent call of educational reform. It was a direct order from those in power, and indirect voices in opposition were barely heard. A vision of change toward better problem-solving skills based on *conceptual* rather than rote learning for *all* of the students was anachronistic, and the voices that promoted it were imperceptible.

Luck was with us! As the world approached and reached the 1990s, rapid changes occurred. The threat of communism was replaced by a growing recession and competition from technologically efficient and achievement-driven European and Asian nations. Parents, who were the baby boom generation, began to wonder if their children would be able to have the same opportunity as they. As a nation and as a school district, we also grappled with changing family structures and the shifting demographics of a repluralized society (Theobold, 1987). In support of my developing vision of better conceptual reasoning skills, as well as equity for the students, came a spate of national reports (e.g., Dossey, Mullis, Lindquist, & Chambers, 1988; McNight et al., 1987). These reports described the disappointing level of student achievement and concluded that "shortages of American scientists, engineers, and technicians are vivid and convincing testimony that our public school system is failing to prepare our people for the future" (Carnegie Commission on Science, Technology and Government, 1991, p. 18). The basics of traditional schooling would not satisfy these needs, nor were they enough to guarantee students their own survival. *All* of the students needed to be better problem solvers and cooperative, informed citizens of the present and future.

"We can be at the vanguard of the movement to meet these needs," I told the district superintendent and board of education. They looked at the falling college board test scores, high school course participation numbers, and test passing rates and agreed—so, for the most part, did the parents. Some teachers were not as responsive. Their perception was that they were already doing everything they could. They believed that the problem was external and unsolvable and saw themselves as powerless victims of these changes in society. The methods they used and values they held had brought them success and satisfaction in the past. It wasn't their fault that today's students wouldn't learn.

A different voice proved significant in helping the teachers accept ownership for themselves of the vision I had presented for our mathematics program. It came a year later from outside our setting but for the most part was accepted by teachers as evolving from their culture. This was the publication of the landmark document *Curriculum and Evaluation Standards for School Mathematics* by the National Council of Teachers of Mathematics, Commission on Standards for School Mathematics (NCTM, 1989b). The council's vision strengthened ours: that *all* of our students would have better number sense (Sowder, 1988, 1992), would become better problem solvers who had confidence in their abilities, and would value mathematics.

The concept that knowledge must be self-constructed became the framework for the accomplishment of our vision and may be one of the most important instructional change outcomes of the restructured schools of the 1990s. I will discuss ideas on constructivism more fully later, but it is important to note here that current definitions imply that each individual constructs his or her own reality and that this reality must fit with human goals and previous perceptions (von Glasersfeld, 1990). This applies not only to students learning mathematics but also to every human adaptation or change of thought. For the same reason, you cannot legislate, you cannot mandate, you cannot expect educational change by just calling for it. Change requires the construction of new knowledge that fits old or new goals or visions. The evocator of change can help this happen, but much depends on the nature of the vision for change itself, the time allotted, and the steps taken.

A new goal or vision of a new future must become part of everyone's own reality before he or she can comfortably accept the rigors of change: The individual must take *ownership*. Verbalizing as one processes information, especially in the peer groups of cooperative learning, has been shown to substantially improve the construction of new knowledge (Slavin, 1983). Giving voice to those who are involved in the process of change may encourage their assumption of ownership of a vision.

Patterson, Purkey, and Parker (1986) address the need for schools to become unbounded from their place and to look beyond themselves with peripheral vision. My colleagues and I soon recognized other voices to consider and saw the need to include parents as critical stakeholders. We engaged them early in our mathematics changes: seeking their opinions in a mailed survey, sharing our goals with letters, and answering their questions at meetings. Then, because some of the parents were suspicious at first, we provided a formal course with hands-on training—and baby-sitting. Their response to this level of involvement had an important impact on the change process. Once convinced, they supported teachers and sometimes pressured them to change as well. Broader involvement by parents in the school management changes came later in the process, presenting a different set of limitations.

Many individuals have visions. Understanding how to give others a voice in visions so that they can be successfully transferred is less common. Although visions were not new to me, I did not always understand how to transfer them.

## Listening to the Voices of Others

In accepting the challenge to manifest an uncharted vision for improving the districtwide instructional program, I had to leave another one behind—one that had begun 7 years earlier. Then, as the new principal of the middle school with a recent doctorate in educational administration, filled with ideas about leadership and organizational development, I made some typical mistakes.

Sergiovanni (1990) describes the successful efforts of new leaders in three steps: bartering, building, and bonding. Starting at the bartering stage in a somewhat hostile, suspicious, and fragmented staff culture, I naively asked for support of my vision for the middle school children (in the form of a mission statement) in exchange for a willingness to listen and a promise to react first to the problems identified as important by the staff. It was not enough to offer—after all, it was my vision and not theirs. Although I was not new to the district, there had not been time to build trust. I still had a lot to learn, and I hadn't taken the time to listen carefully to the voices around me. Fortunately, I soon had some help. It began with Tom.

I had worked closely with Tom before. He and I had begun new ventures at the same time, Tom as a middle school math teacher appointed to the assistant principalship and I as a high school science teacher beginning my career as a science coordinator. Tom was one of the most admired and loved teachers in the district. He had actually grown up in our suburban yet small-town-like community of South Vale, and his own children attended the local schools. His summer job as assistant manager at the local swim club made him a well-recognized and appreciated member of the whole community. As a classroom teacher, and even as a soccer coach, his approach was patient, warm, and gentle, but firm.

There were no bad kids in Tom's classes. After many years of experience, he still wrote careful uncollected lesson plans and was always there when a school job needed to be done. His "free time" was usually spent in the classroom with kids who needed extra help or just wanted to be around him. Tom's administrative career lasted only one year. "I can't stand the nonsense," he explained, "and I miss being in the classroom with the kiddies." That did not mean he would stop growing. His classroom was filled with new ideas, and he was a critical opinion leader in the mathematics changes to come.

In my first few months at the middle school, Tom gave me some important insights. He explained the philosophical differences between the elementary-certified sixth-grade teachers and the secondary-minded eighth-grade teachers and their consequent mistrust of each other. This helped me understand why my first attempt to improve the schedule, which began with only the eighth grade, was met with anger by many of the staff. The changes, which I hoped eventually would be schoolwide, resulted in some extra preparation time for the eighth-grade teachers. I had shared my rationale for beginning at this grade level: Extra instructional time was needed for the students who were taking high school-level advanced courses. But the staff had not really been involved in the decision and did not understand that I was given only limited resources for the changes by the district office. My background as a high school teacher didn't help—the elementary teachers thought I was partial to the secondary-level purposes.

In any case, the staff had been quite comfortable with their fatherly and handsome previous principal and had also grown to love their charismatic young assistant principal. They were disappointed that he hadn't been promoted into the new position. Female secondary principals were not yet in their role model comfort zone. "You won't prove yourself to us until you get into that auditorium at lunchtime with 500 screaming kids and get some order," one of the eighth-grade teachers told me. That was what the whole staff had in common—an abhorrence of lunch duty.

## Bartering, Building, and Bonding

Well, if lunchtime supervision made teachers feel that they were less than professionals, then that is where I needed to begin! I had found something to barter for their trust. We cut the time for the students' lunch period to 30 minutes, and after some fervent negotiation with central office (there was little site-based control of funds or staffing), we replaced the missing activity time with a period of physical education every day. I assigned students to seats and made sure the rules that the teachers, the children, and I developed together were followed. My own presence and follow-through made the final difference and was fair exchange for some beginning trust.

As trust began to grow, I bartered more seriously. Tom had been helpful in explaining my mistakes and in preventing others. Why not ask others to help as well? I took some risk and invited the staff to evaluate me as their leader in exchange for their involvement in school decision making. They didn't know me well enough to feel comfortable with this at first, even when I promised anonymity. But we formed the "professional growth committee," and Tom was joined by Sandy and several others.

The building process followed. Together the committee and I planned for tightening up other loose ends, such as the rest of the schedule that no one liked and the behavior of the kids in assemblies, in the halls, and at dismissals. We cleaned up the graffiti and changed the report cards. We set up systems for sharing our expectations with the students and rewarding them for meeting them. A student mediation team was organized to help settle minor disputes and infractions of school rules.

The committee helped me select two new assistant principals and several new teachers and teaching assistants. After committee members participated in interviews, I asked not for their preference but for their acceptance or nonacceptance of each candidate—and never hired anyone who was not acceptable. We planned rewards for ourselves as well, some of them social and some professional. Each month we issued a written newsletter, the *Pride Periodical*, which highlighted the productive and innovative things individuals were doing in school, as well as in their personal lives.

In our seventh year together, evidence of bonding, shared values, and commitment showed in the entire staff's willingness to cooperatively develop new experiences for kids, including a 3-day outdoor

# Understanding the Roles of Visions and Voices

experience away from school. It also showed in staff members' acceptance of a negative tenure decision and a series of budget cuts, in growing pride in the school, and in their humor and good spirits instead of complaints in the informal forum: their lunchroom.

The middle school had been the underdog, the zoo; now many teachers wanted to work there. Community perception also grew more positive. The building shone because everyone cared, and this caring was transmitted to the kids. Not everything was perfect, by far; pockets of isolation and mistrust still existed. We paid no attention to the quantitative evaluation of instructional effectiveness. Nor had we even approached, as a collegial group, the need for change in instructional process.

Just as we needed to get to this, the school district moved into a more formal systemwide design for school improvement that included site-based collaborative management. The design involved principals, teachers, and other staff members in a shared planning and decision-making process. I will refer to this vision as site-based collaborative decision making (SBCDM).

## Developing a Systemic Vision for School Improvement

This new plan for school improvement was initiated by the district central office with board of education sponsorship in the spring of 1987. I was never quite sure at the time whose vision it actually was. I knew that our superintendent had knowledge of a school district within the state that was in the process of implementing a program improvement design in response to the "effective schools" literature.[2] This literature, which was based on a limited body of research, was quite prominent in the late 1980s. It related several characteristics of schools to their effectiveness (as judged by students' test performance). This particular program design was different and appealing to some of us because it emphasized the involvement of teachers and other staff in the improvement process.

The superintendent arranged a visit by a group of board of education members, the assistant superintendent, teachers (including union leaders), and curriculum directors (but no principals) to that school district. Impressed with what they saw, these opinion leaders showed interest in possible replication of the project. As so often happens, each individual viewed the new situation from a personal perspective or, as the constructivists would say, constructed his or her own reality. The board members and central office administrators saw achieving the effective schools criteria as the predominant program goal with the collaborative management implementation structure as the means to an end. The teachers saw collaborative management as the program goal and lightly dismissed the significance of the effective schools criteria. This difference of perspective was often discussed at meetings of the administrative council, but nonetheless it prevailed throughout most of the first years—and created problems.

The other principals and I felt somewhat left out. Although I appreciated the concept of participative management (as described previously, I was engaged in it myself), careful perusal of the effective schools criteria revealed some cognitive conflicts. How could one get strong administrative leadership in a collaborative culture? Leadership for the restructuring process itself was tenuous. Although the superintendent and board of education seemed committed, they did little to demonstrate or develop their vision. They placed responsibility for the effort with the assistant superintendent, who was replaced within 3 months by Peter, one of the curriculum directors.

Peter quickly engaged a nationally recognized outside consultant to help get the program launched. In a brief but intensive visit, the consultant shared his message with the entire school community, beginning with building administrators and then addressing teachers and parents in small and large groups. His charisma, the support of the teachers' union, and the promise of a new, stronger decision-making role for staff provided just the right combination of *evocator* motivations for us to consider change. This is a common way for school districts to initiate change. A highly motivating person comes in, gets everyone perked up, and then disappears. No one is left to pick up the slack, to deal with the many unexpected difficulties, and to generate new energy when the going gets tough.

The original district improvement plan was developed by a district leadership team (DLT) composed of the principals, a teacher representing each school, Peter (in his new role as assistant to the superintendent), and the union president and vice presidents. The plan was composed in a pleasant, away-from-school setting in a concentrated 3-day marathon. As middle school principal, I was

# Understanding the Roles of Visions and Voices 29

present at this beginning and remember being inspired by the combined energies and excitement of sharing goals, hopes, and aspirations. Agreement was not always easy, and I was proud of Peter (who had started out as my assistant principal) as he helped the group reach consensus.

Everyone was committed to the ideas of improvement and the involvement of the entire staff, but the focus on outcomes that depended on the state-mandated and standardized tests was less understood and somehow underemphasized in our discussions. This was unfortunate, because I don't think the teachers ever realized or accepted the bottom line of test-based accountability for this vision. They listened selectively to its opportunity to become involved in decision making and did not absorb the connected acceptance of responsibility. I will discuss the importance of consensus, commitment, and focus on outcomes in Chapter 7.

We brainstormed ideas, but Peter wrote the formal plan—and it stretched the accountability part. The plan included acceptance of the effective schools criteria as improvement goals, which would help us reach districtwide standards that were based on improved socioeconomically disaggregated test scores.[3] The plan declared our equity-seeking grounding mission that "all children can and will learn." It also designed the structure of the individual building leadership teams (BLTs). We had a vision, and seemingly some of the most influential people in the school district were committed to it!

Typically, however, only one of the principals present at this time of initial commitment was destined to follow through as a team member for more than a year. Peter left soon afterward and a new assistant superintendent (the third) was assigned to coordinate the restructuring effort. Nontenured replacement administrators who were not present for this original commitment may have had an effect on the rate of reform, at least for the first few years. There must be some cognitive dissonance for a new principal, anxious to establish himself or herself as a leader, who is simultaneously charged to accept someone else's vision, especially one that requires an abdication of some power. Inconsistency of leadership vision is an ongoing difficulty in schools. Administrators are usually people with upwardly mobile careers who move around. The remedy for this is to have strong collegial cultures with consensus of vision and involvement of teacher-leaders in the selection of administrators (see Chapters 4 and 8).

## Perceiving Visions for School Reform

The district's significant effort to restructure schools was based on a complex vision that required profound people change. As it often happens, this vision was presumed to be singular and clear. It was not, although everyone's view had SBCDM in sight. Teachers saw the participative management system as the end: a true change in formal culture. Administrators saw the change in decision making as a better way to reach the outcome of more effective schools, as measured by better performance by students on standardized tests.

This difference is echoed in the literature calling for educational reform. Like the underlying vision of the district administrative staff, Finn (1990) suggests, affirmatively, that the direction of change will demand a new definition of education as "the result achieved," rather than the process, intention, or investment. He projects a complicated "paradigm shift," requiring major restructuring and diverse approaches to reaching outcomes (p. 586).

Lieberman and Miller (1990), on the other hand, see the restructuring process more as our teachers did and identify five building blocks of the restructuring process:

1. A rethinking of curricular and instructional efforts to promote quality and equality for all students
2. A rethinking of the structure of the school
3. A two-pronged focus on a rich learning environment for students and on a professionally supported work environment for teachers
4. A recognition of the necessity for building partnerships and networks
5. A recognition of the increased and changing participation of parents and teachers (p. 761)

Although the district's initiation of change predates the suggestions described above, we were fortunate to have simultaneous visions for program change and total school improvement with a plan for site-based collaborative management. We also had the unique opportunity to incorporate each of these building blocks with varying levels of success. Singly, perhaps, the effect of some seemed less than significant. Viewed holistically, as a new structure with the blocks supporting each other, the result was a system of much greater strength than ever before. The process of transforming a vision into reality, however, was not easy.

# Understanding the Roles of Visions and Voices 31

The problems with the change to site-based management began with the lack of congruence of its vision. Although there was a shared mission statement, it meant different things to different people. That "all children can and will learn" meant to the teachers that they would have new power to meet this imperative of their working lives—the one that brought them the greatest rewards. To others in power, it meant that they would hand over some of the accountability for meeting that mission to teachers—accountability but not real power. This is a symptom of "loosely coupled" organizations such as schools (Weick, 1976, p. 1). Different parts of the organization have different ends in mind, but they proceed and accept the silent acquiescence of the others, especially those not in power, as approval. And then they lunge ahead!

## Visions as Starting and Ending Places

When the starting gate is opened, the flag is dropped, or the pistol is shot, not everyone gets off to a smooth beginning. Some falter or fumble, but everyone is running on the same track and knows where the finish line is. Visions can get educators started, but in schools we may need to run together, or at least toward the same worthy end. Visions also don't tell us much about how to run the race. Like our track-bound counterparts, some of us forge ahead at full speed toward our envisioned goal, indiscriminately leaving others behind or pushing them aside. Others bide their time, getting to know the voices and the strengths and weaknesses of the others in the race. Neither approach guarantees success. There are too many variables, and humans do not respond well to being pushed aside. In schools we can't afford to leave anyone behind—so the lunge approach may not be the best. We need to listen and to plan our strategies well.

On the other hand, a good leader sets the pace and drives everyone to perform his or her best. If a leader drops off, however, there had better be a new one with the same destination in mind. In our district's case, we embarked on the manifestation of two different visions that were meant to end up as one. Although they were separate at the start and differently realized, their paths did cross and their energies were combined. Even after 7 years, however, they have not yet converged.

Perhaps those of us who want to improve schools need multiple or incremental ways to reach our visions and multiple tracks to run on, as long as we are reaching for the same winner's circle and don't collide. If we fail at one, all is not lost. Understanding why we win some races and lose others may also help us and others in the future. Even losing a race may not be all bad if progress was made and lessons were learned. South Vale has not lost either race yet—but it could. Maybe others, who learn what happened to us, will win theirs!

Each race, however, is unique; the experience of the runners is different, the track is different, and the time is different. These must be considered and responded to. The next chapter explores the role of history and setting in the steeplechase of improving schools.

## Notes

1. For the Kpelle, see Gay and Cole (1967). For the Vai and Gola, see Lave (1977). For the Dioula and the Baoule, see Ginsburg, Posner, and Russell (1981).

2. For the ideas of effective schools, see Edmonds (1983) and Rutter, Maughan, Mortimer, Ouston, and Smith (1979).

3. Disaggregation of test scores was effected by separating students into two groups according to the level of education of their mothers. Because of the relative homogeneity of the population, this was the only viable distinction for assessing whether or not our program made a difference and for ensuring that the results were not dependent on the socioeconomic status of the student. In essence, we wanted to know if it worked for all students.

# 3

# Knowing the Setting and Its History

### About This Chapter

The events that compose the initiation of systemic change can be construed as the building of new settings, but they are usually built on an old foundation. Just as visions project the future, history looks at the past. Sarason (1972) has reminded us that "confronting its [the setting's] history for the purpose of dealing with it was crucial for its future" (p. 63). Even the present, which seems so apparent, is in effect the result of the past. The building of new settings, therefore, needs to begin with a critical and in-depth analysis of the present. Such an analysis may provide a rationale for that confrontation. This chapter demonstrates how careful attention to history and setting prepares a system for successful implementation of change and how history itself can influence success.

### The Role of History

As historians and literary futurists such as Wells, Huxley, and Dickens suggest, the ability to predict and control the future may be limited—human behavior is particularly unpredictable—but it is by no means immutable. To take some hold of the future, however, it is important to understand the events and conditions that fashioned the past and control the present. Changing a school requires knowledge of the political, social, and historical context of the place and also, perhaps, that one must be "a true believer" in the worth of the enterprise (Smith, Prunty, Dwyer, & Kleine, 1986, p. 91).

Deal (1990) argues that people must "treat educational organizations as complex social organisms held together by symbolic webbing" and that "history tells us that tinkering with formal roles and relationships will not make a significant difference in the lives of teachers and students" (p. 7). He offers two alternatives: one requiring a look backward to the effective practices in the past and the other requiring a metamorphosis or refocus.

I agree with Deal about tinkering, but my experiences do not tell me that his alternatives are mutually exclusive approaches to productive change—especially when the look at the past includes the personal, social, and political history of the organization as well as the successful practices of the past. The challenge in examining history is to discern which values and systems of the past can be appropriately transmitted into the present and future, which need to be transformed, and which should be systematically abandoned. *The restructuring of the future, however, must be based on a carefully evaluated retrospective.* History is another voice to be heard.

Like the other affecting variables of change, history does not stand by itself. It interacts with ownership, power, capacity, vision, and the others. The thread of history entwined itself into both strengthening and encumbering knots as we implemented our innovations at South Vale, or as Smith et al. (1986) would identify them, specific planned changes in mathematics education in the midst of a broad-based school reform effort to improve the schools with SBCDM.

## Transforming and Transmitting History: An Example

Let us consider my vision for the changes in mathematics as an example. The recognition of the importance of building new formal knowledge from the reservoir of informal problem-solving skills already possessed by the students was in response to what others learned from cross-cultural studies of more primitive societies and from my own reflections and those of my peers on the more concrete

# Knowing the Setting and Its History

experiences of children in the past. We late-20th-century educators are not the first to recognize the value of rational applications to real-life problems—or of the encouragement of original solutions.

In 1866, Maglathlin published his text titled *Greenleaf's New Practical Arithmetic*. In his introduction, with the terseness of an era in which print and paper were expensive, he describes his work as

> developing principles by inductive methods, deducing rules from rational solutions, and encouraging self-reliance and originality by numerous exercises in analysis . . . keeping prominently in view the practical uses of numbers, by various applications of a business character. While it avoids obsolete or useless material, it properly treats new topics requiring attention, such as the metric system of weights and measures, annual interest, internal revenue; and enforces thorough educational results. . . . Without a knowledge of these principles, the art of using numbers becomes mere mechanical ciphering. (p. 6)

With an update on the language, this could describe the direction of the changes at South Vale. We heeded his advice to add what is now new (besides metrics, interest, and internal revenue) and considered the demands for problem-solving abilities in a new technological world. The redundant drill and practice that developed the skills of speed and accuracy for complex computations, necessary in a time gone by but in the present obsolete, would have to be *transformed* to better reasoning skills. Maglathlin's philosophy and understanding of the learning process, however, were worthy of *transmission*.

It is a pity that these ideas were subverted by generations of rote learning of mathematics and by the confusing disruption of the post-*Sputnik* new math—an approach neither designed by nor ever really accepted by teachers (Kilpatrick, 1985). The mathematicians who designed these programs hoped to solve all problems by top-down inculcation of a new method in which the children would learn general principles and then apply these deductively to the computations and problems of mathematics. Unfortunately, in practice, these principles were memorized by rote (by teachers and their students) and applied without meaning. Although they were sound principles, useful to mathematicians, the programs completely ignored what Maglathlin instinctively knew and teachers had learned from Piaget: Children learn inductively from informal and formal structured experiences that lead them to the construction of their own concepts and principles (Piaget, 1977; Polya, 1981).

For the math teachers and parents in South Vale, the unfulfilled promise of the new math was the greatest hurdle of history to overcome. Our beginning task in implementing change was related to this history. Knowing that we had a generation of adults who were taught in this manner and that parents and teachers teach the way they learned (Lortie, 1975), we would have to reteach them first!

## Documenting History: Listening to Its Voices

Many of us who were innovators in the past remember a frequently offered suggestion: New leaders get a honeymoon period for change in which resistance is diminished because change is expected. This was probably true, but the diminution in resistance did not automatically ensure the assumption of ownership—especially if the innovation contradicted the values, habits, and reward systems of the culture. As I have discussed in the preceding chapter, new leaders with visions often blindly lunge from the starting gate, unconscious and insensitive to the condition of the track and the nature of the cultural adversaries. They don't take the time to listen to the voices of the others in the race. Some of the voices we listened to in our district may resemble some that you have heard.

"There's too much going on in this district at one time—why can't we focus just on the math or just on the building management plans?" was a common lament heard from teachers and administrators in South Vale. Greta, an elementary teacher about whom we will learn more in the next chapter, readily expressed her experience-based rationale for not participating in our formal math in-service program or serving on her BLT:

> It will all go away with the next new administrator or President's report. I've been teaching math this way for years—and kids still need to know their tables. Lots of drill and practice are what they need. Some kids just are not born to be good at it. And as for teachers on building leadership teams—those administrators will never let us make real decisions. They just like to make us do their work!

# Knowing the Setting and Its History

Overloads of top-down imposed innovations with little real effort to build teachers' capacity to use or sustain them have been a real problem for schools in the past. They especially affect elementary teachers, who must deal with all of the subjects and a constantly changing cadre of central office and building administrators. Unfortunately, educators have often impulsively reacted to some new promise of a better way, usually with poorly researched evidence of effectiveness and scant regard for what has already happened or for how a change is related to something else. South Vale did have a curriculum cycle that was supposed to prevent this, but new incumbents with their own priorities sometimes disrupted it.

Some teachers who were veterans of these vicissitudes reacted openly and negatively to the new proposals for reform; others sat smugly on the sidelines with knowing disinterest. Some raised their voices in compliant and hopeful support and faced the derision of cynical colleagues. Several shared their own perspectives of the problems they faced and enlightened us about the difficulties we would need to overcome. Gary was such an informer.

## Gary

Gary, a high school math teacher, had been with the district for more than 25 years. When we first met, he was assigned to a physics class, and I was a new science teacher. I remember being quite impressed with his knowledge in both fields. He lived in a much larger neighboring school district in which his own two children were highly successful students in fast-tracked classes. Gary was a good mathematician and worked conscientiously with his students, but he had some rigid attitudes about who was going to succeed and where the blame for failure was. He had no compunctions about blaming his elementary school colleagues, parents, or the students themselves. I was pleased when Gary volunteered to join the math needs assessment committee. He was the only high school math department member on it. The other high school teacher was a chemistry teacher who taught math courses.

At our meetings, Gary was often confrontational; I also noticed that in informal settings, he was sometimes teased by his colleagues, who liked to provoke him. But at least he was honest and forthright about his feelings; we needed to hear his story. In the past, Gary had often been assigned to teach the geometry courses that no one else desired because of the "extra work" marking proofs. Only rarely had he been assigned to the upper-level or accelerated classes he would have preferred. On the other hand, although he frequently worked excitedly with individual students while supervising study hall or lunch, he was not considered patient with "slow learners."

Gary commented with conviction at the first meeting of the math needs assessment committee: "Most of the kids in our school district are more interested in sports than in academics—or else they just want to work at the local supermarket so they can buy clothes and a car. They don't know their basic facts, either, when they get to the high school." The school district did have a reputation for its jocks rather than for its scholars. A group of parents and staff certainly supported these values. The sports program was admired and well funded, but attempts to promote special academic programs for the more capable students were often labeled elitist. The staff believed that our students were mostly "average kids," and we thought we were doing our best for the large middle group. But perhaps our expectations for this majority of the students were not what they should have been. Some of the parents were beginning to believe this, too.

## Jean Brown

One of these parents, Jean Brown, made the following remark when interviewed about changes she would like to see: "I think the middle of the road children need to be concentrated on a little more. I thought about that after we talked about programs we have for gifted and for handicapped and what they are doing" (Westervelt, 1993, p. 151).[1]

Mrs. Brown is the parent of three children in the school district; the oldest is a high school student. She moved to the district from New York City because "everything is so big there." Jean learned about the district from a neighbor, who did a great deal of research and selected South Vale. At first she sent her younger children to the local parochial school but soon shifted them to the public school. Although the school system was not the only deciding factor, Jean stated that "to us it is the biggest investment we will ever make. . . .

# Knowing the Setting and Its History

Given everything, it was someplace we thought would be suitable to live." Like many parents in this country, Jean had a 3-day-a-week job, but she did become involved in the PTA and in the building leadership team. I will come back to her in later chapters. For now, it may be useful to know more about the context of these voices.

## The School District: The Context of Change

The school culture setting in which these voices were heard as we at South Vale began the transformation to SBCDM and the reform in mathematics education may be typical of many school systems: bounded in the past or present, hardened by a parade of top-down incursions that made little difference, and isolated from the dynamic societal changes that unrelentingly and inevitably must control them. It wasn't that we didn't attempt to deal with this. We always searched for a better way! We had tried, for example, open classrooms, direct instruction, instructional management programs, initial teaching alphabet, career education, and many new texts. Most of these were superficial top-down impositions that were abandoned when leadership faltered or was replaced, and teachers quickly reverted to the old methods they found more comfortable.

The history of other more recent attempts at change that were based on hopeful but poorly documented and transitory efforts to link cognitive research and the learning process was another hurdle to overcome because these efforts failed to ring true or be implementable in a typical classroom. For example, after a dynamic presentation and some follow-up workshops in the 1980s, the district had responded (with little success) to a flurry of research on right and left brain dominance differences. The prescriptions for our teachers to recognize and respond to differences in student learning styles were difficult—we did little to build their capacity—and they were *untimely*. They were incongruous with a concurrent "back to basics" movement and a rigid set of state-mandated standards outlined as *The Regents Action Plan* (University of the State of New York, 1984).

Conflicting double-bind schizophrenic messages such as these make teachers wary of top-down imposed and often inadequately researched change efforts, dooming them to failure. These failures cast an additional veil of suspicion on any incursion on the teachers' prevailing pedagogical base: a foundation acquired through the years from the previous messages of experts, strengthened by their own habits of mind and practice, and confirmed by broad public acceptance. Readers will see other examples of this in the chapters ahead.

The district had some notable successes, such as the elementary science program that had a permanent impact on how this subject was taught, but it, too, was subject to the damages of time and changing leadership. Much of the vision and energy for the district's innovations of the past had come from a 25-year history of subject area coordinators whose roles were then consolidated into those of the central office-based curriculum directors. The directors were responsible for budgeting for districtwide programs and also usually managed the cyclic review of curriculum that customarily began with a formal needs assessment. This structure essentially removed much of the money and program power out of the individual buildings and was not changed for the first 5 years of site-based management! The variable history of the sources of power may have predicted the differential success of the changes in curriculum and governance in South Vale. Applying this to school districts in general, shifts to SBCDM may be most difficult in districts in which central office curriculum staff have been traditional holders of power.

The superintendent of the district when our changes began had been there for more than 15 years—not the usual tenure for superintendents. He had come to the district 3 years after I began there as a high school teacher, but my career as an administrator began with his arrival. Almost all of the other administrative staff had been there for less than 5 years. Our district was a place for beginners to gain experience to move on to bigger and better places. Leadership turnover may be vitalizing in inspiring new vision, but a history of it eventually becomes dysfunctional because the lack of consistency makes teachers insecure, jaded, and impervious to new incursions. Only careful listening to voices, trust, and vision building can overcome this historical cultural constraint.

In contrast, when the district began the change efforts, the teaching staff was mature and, as a result of strong union leadership in the expansion years of the 1960s and early 1970s, was well paid by national standards. The population of South Vale had declined during the 1980s but is on its way up again. In the late 1980s, there were only two K-4 elementary schools, a 5-7 middle school, and one 8-12 high school, each with its own principal. Declining enrollment had caused the excessing of most of the younger staff, another variable of history that affected both changes. A slight differential between the relative seniorities of the staffs of the two elementary schools helped identify the significance of this variable. In 1991, a retirement incentive and a trend toward higher enrollment began a whole new phase that brought the benefits and needs of many new teachers, as well as some interesting and unpredicted connections of this history, to the variables of power and leadership.

I will explore these further in later chapters, but a preliminary observation here is that the relative career stages of teachers will affect the implementation of change. Not surprisingly, younger teachers will be more receptive, but they may also not be ready to take over the responsibilities and risks of teacher-leadership.

The student population of South Vale was gradually changing from rather homogeneously White to larger representations of different cultures, particularly Asians. Although a popular and successful local parochial school siphoned off some of the Catholic children, this group formed a population majority in the town that was reflected in the culture of our students. Many other religions, including those of Eastern origin, were represented by a house of worship within the district boundaries—some even shared the same house. One or two incidents of anti-Semitic vandalism had occurred during the preceding 20 years. In general, however, nothing disturbed the overt tranquility of the community for long.

The socioeconomic distribution was also becoming more diverse: Small pockets of upper-middle-class families appeared in juxtaposition with second- and third-generation civil servants and a spatter of new immigrants. The main street in town was gradually losing business to the larger malls. The American Legion, Masons, Rotary, Knights of Columbus, Hibernians, and Elks all had local chapters with strong memberships. A powerful local newspaper made South Vale seem more like a midwestern town than an eastern suburb. But the fire companies, ambulance corps, and scouts complained bitterly about the lack of volunteers because everyone in the family was working to keep up. Many of the students worked at the local stores or nearby malls, often for extended and illegal hours. Not until we started to check our records carefully for differences in socioeconomic status did we also realize from how many nontraditional families the children came.

The culture from which our children came to school in the mid-1980s may have been different, but if 50-year-old visitors closed their eyes so that they couldn't see the computer or the reams of copy sheets, they would be right back in their own third grade. Despite all our efforts to innovate, with the exception of the introduction of computers (and these remained peripheral to most of the instructional process), teaching methods and relationships among the professionals and with their client parents were hardly different from what they had been 30, 40, or 50 years ago—as they are in so many other places in this country. Getting a budget passed, winning statewide sports titles, keeping standardized test scores up, and making children and parents happy with the status quo were more important than thinking about the future—its unpredictability, moreover, seemed threatening.

Comments about the lack of emphasis on academic excellence were often made by parents and teachers, but hearing them from the local real estate agents made them even more disturbing. Despite the above-average student IQ scores, good performance on competency tests, and a high per-pupil expenditure, the real estate agents were directing parents who were in search of strongly academic school systems to neighboring districts. The lower-than-expected College Board SAT scores and the disappointing number of diplomas with a Regents endorsement signifying completion of a program of academic courses were evidence that they may have been right.

## Documenting History and Setting: A Template

Oral history has its place, and those who live within a culture and pay attention to it have a pretty good idea about its nature. But every observer's perception is subject to his or her previously held realities and values. Needs assessments have traditionally been used to systematically examine and document the results of history. A well-done needs assessment can serve many purposes. It can

- Connect the present to the past and the future
- Codify and verify the many different voices in the culture
- Uncover hidden misconceptions, prejudices, concerns, and needs
- Correct perceptions and misconceptions
- Create just enough disequilibrium to alert some of us to consider change

# Knowing the Setting and Its History

- Collate voices and set the stage for building consensus
- Communicate visions and values

Needs assessments are unfortunately sometimes misapplied. They cannot be done long distance; they require careful planning and legwork. Closed-ended instruments do not allow for voices to be heard and can force an outcome that is invalid for the reality of what is assessed. In that respect, they have the same problems that many find with traditional tests. An authentic needs assessment requires some degree of openendedness. The danger of too much of this, of course, is that the data may then be difficult to define.

My solution to this dilemma is to start in an open-ended way with a representative and fair-sized needs assessment working group that during a reasonable period shares and explores the past, the present, and possibilities for the future. On the basis of these open-ended discoveries, the group can develop a set of values or, as the present *zeitgeist* calls them, standards; then they can design a variety of closed- and open-ended instruments to test the many voices and to document what they believe exists.

## Assessing Needs for School Improvement

The needs assessment that prepared us at South Vale for SBCDM did only some of this. I described the formation of our DLT in the preceding chapter, but a review of the compressed time perspective is critical here. The original DLT met for the first time just a few weeks after the visit of the outside consultant. Within 2 or 3 weeks after our planning meeting, the original district plan was shared with the entire staff. The DLT did not see the written document until that time. It was close to the end of the school year, and each building hastily elected its own BLT composed of teachers, principal, and other staff members including teaching assistants, secretaries, and custodians (parent membership did not come until the fourth year).

As I discussed in the previous chapter, the visions of the teachers and the administrators and board were not the same. No open-ended needs assessment was done to help clarify the visions or to discover whether a change in school management was desired or even whether people felt that improvement was necessary at all. Nevertheless, the

DLT had generated much enthusiasm, and although the skeptics still represented a large minority, we plunged rapidly into an externally designed closed-ended assessment that looked for the specifics of assumed needs. We were on our way to a change in school culture—at least that is what many of the teachers believed! From their perspective, this was just the first step toward SBCDM.

The instrument we used was a survey designed around the effective schools criteria. It was developed by the New York State Education Department, which was at that time committed to this optimistic design for improving schools. None of us (except for Peter, the assistant to the superintendent) had seen the survey beforehand, and it was administered to everyone in large groups at the same time. Questions were asked in each of 10 categories: positive school climate, planning process, academic goals/high expectations, clearly defined curricula, teacher/staff effectiveness, administrative leadership, parent and community involvement, opportunities for student responsibility and participation, rewards and incentives, and order and discipline.

Although the survey was based on the already determined criteria for effective schools, it did allow for each individual to denote a personal opinion of the degree of importance for each criterion and then the degree of its existence. Observations of teachers completing the survey showed that some, either bored or caring little, just indiscriminately filled in blanks. Others belabored every choice. "Whose vision was this, anyway!" Although the survey questioned the importance and existence of collegial relationships and planning, it never defined SBCDM, suggested how such decisions might be made, or considered where the source of power resides.

## Planning for Improvement

All of the BLTs met in one place for the first time in the summer of 1987. After some preparatory explanation of the task to the entire group, the individual BLTs separated to respond to the results of the needs assessment. They identified those areas in which the discrepancies between desired and existing conditions were the greatest and then wrote school improvement plans with activities designed to correct these discrepancies. Each team also wrote a mission statement. The combination of the plan and statement became the team's visions for change.

# Knowing the Setting and Its History

Everyone was in high spirits. No one seemed to realize that everything was generated by a closed-ended survey, which probably missed some important issues. The areas diagnosed as deficient varied with the building and level. The planning process, academic goals and high expectations, and rewards and incentives were first-time priorities for more than one school. For every school except the middle school, developing a positive school climate seemed most important. At the high school, as in many in this country, order and discipline were also identified as in need of improvement. The high school BLT responded to these needs with optimistic plans including new discipline procedures, but a major focus for the high school team soon became their role in the selection of a new principal. None of the schools, perhaps because of traditional lack of trust, chose improving leadership as a priority.

Then still a building principal, I recall decided apprehension about how the teachers would judge my administrative leadership. The formal survey seemed to be threatening, perhaps because it was essentially externally imposed and in some ways contradictory. Nobody had bothered to review the progress with participative management that we had already made. Would my previous attempts to implement shared decision making be viewed as less than strong leadership? They were not, and because of this history, positive school climate was not identified as a priority by the middle school teachers. Their reasons were stated in their plan for the 1987-1988 school year:

> For this year we have decided not to focus on this area because based on the data, the staff feels that the middle school is a safe, secure, attractive place to work. In the building there is high staff morale where teachers treat students fairly and consistently and the classroom atmosphere is conducive to learning.

It was comforting for me to know this, but comfort and complacency may not be the best environment for change. In such situations, a leader may have to create some disequilibrium. The middle school would have a new leader (I left to become curriculum director), and new leaders may not be able to take the risk of creating disequilibrium. These may have been variables that deprived the middle school staff of some necessary continuing momentum for the further growth of their collegial culture (see Chapters 6 and 8). They chose to focus on clearly defined curricula—a logical next step—and planned interdisciplinary activities and assessment of the curriculum for continuity and collaborative planning. The middle school team was an exception: The area of clearly defined curricula was addressed only tangentially this first year by the other teams.

The historical organization of K-12 curriculum-based program elements managed by central office directors was not considered at all in the first site-based plans. Traditionally, separate—often vertical (K-12) and interschool—committees had dealt with curriculum issues, with directors of curriculum filling the major, but not isolated, administrative role on these committees. It was just such a committee that began that same year to explore the state of the district's mathematics program.

## Tracking Down History and Needs

It was my responsibility, in my new position as the curriculum director, to lead this exploration. Legwork, or wandering around, can be both supportive and informative to the evocator of change, especially to avoid lunging into visions. In frequent visits to elementary school classrooms during the first 6 months, I rarely saw mathematics being taught. Yet teachers said they spent time on math. The time was mostly used for drill and practice activities from texts, workbooks, or ditto sheets with the children working at their seats alone or at the teacher's desk as their work was corrected. There were brief periods of whole group direct instruction, but interactive whole or small group discourse in math was practically nonexistent. Only isolated use of manipulatives was evident, although some teachers had a few.

Essentially, the existing mathematics program at the elementary and middle school levels consisted of a textbook series. Teachers methodically "covered" the material and used expendable workbooks to supplement the text's already redundant drill and practice activities. Sometimes motivated students were encouraged to go beyond their grade levels, completing the texts and workbooks but frequently not really understanding the underlying concepts and often not prepared for the more abstract problems of high school math.

With the exception of the introduction of metrics and a focus on measurement in the mid-1970s, no mathematics curriculum change

# Knowing the Setting and Its History

or major staff development had occurred at the elementary level for more than 20 years. For the most part, elementary teachers seemed satisfied that they were doing a good job teaching math. They were reassured by the successful performance of students on state-mandated basic competency tests and the locally selected California Achievement Tests (CATs), which were above the national norms.

The New York State Education Department recommends a specific curriculum in most high school subject areas that is evaluated by statewide tests named after its governing body, the Board of Regents. Courses that prepare students for these exams are usually academically challenging and are considered by most parents and teachers as the standard for college preparation. Students who do not pass the required Regents exams may not receive a valued Regents endorsement on their diplomas—even if they pass the courses. The public reporting of these test results heightened mathematics teachers' concerns about who was placed in Regents courses, and much energy was expended on making recommendations for student placement in and out of the Regents track. The teachers viewed these courses as too difficult for a large number of our students and therefore had always supported a variety of locally modified classes. A nonrepeating ninth grader, for example, could be found in at least five different tracks. There were also special classes for nonmainstreamed special education students.

The successful performance of elementary and middle school students on basic competency tests and CATs in no measure presaged the lack of success of students in math at the high school level. Less than 40% of the students went on to a third year of Regents high school math. In the year before the change process began, only 59% of these students, or 24% of the total third-year class, actually passed the Regents exam. Results on the SAT were at or slightly above national averages but did not compare favorably with similar neighboring districts. High school teachers blamed the lack of student achievement on poor preparation, lack of motivation, and lack of mathematical talent. A much clearer focus on the reasons for this discrepancy in measured student achievement was needed.

## Getting Started in an Open-Ended Way

In February of the first year of implementation of the program improvement plans—which at that time concentrated on organizational and school climate needs—I initiated the task of involving teachers in a separate collegial cluster, whose objective was to explore the needs of the mathematics program. Because so many other collegial cluster activities were simultaneously being conducted, my original request for volunteer staff involvement on the math team carefully constructed the *time* commitment (see Patterson et al., 1986). Teachers are protective of their time and are especially wary of time spent at unproductive meetings. Payment for extra time had been an incentive for some of the work of the district and building teams (although far from covering it all), but no money was offered for participation in this math needs assessment cluster. This lack of compensation (either in time or extra money) for the time and energy teachers use in shared planning and decision making diminishes its apparent value. It is only in the education profession that effort expended in the accomplishment of mutual goals is undervalued. Businesspersons and other professionals build time for it into the workday (see Chapter 8).

The invitation to participate in the needs assessment was accompanied by a copy of a recent newspaper article that provided a brief introductory rationale for the effort. It organized the process into three steps: a consensual determination of what should be, what is, and what needs to be done (Zakariya, 1983). It also provided a limited schedule of after-school meeting dates. The response to my invitation was encouraging. Twenty staff members (out of a possible 44 directly involved in math instruction) became involved. Included were 3 building principals, 2 high school teachers (including Gary), 4 middle school teachers, 10 elementary teachers, and a teaching assistant. Several BLT members were also in the group. This provided a nucleus for staff ownership and a vehicle for the needed leadership support structure.

For the first meeting, I had planned to provide some of our local and national data as a background for further discussion and to develop some general goals (what should be), but the relevant facts provoked heated exchanges between elementary and secondary teachers—each placing the blame for disappointing student performance on the other. The high school teachers openly attributed it to poor elementary preparation, as well as to lack of talent, parent indifference, and inadequate student motivation to achieve. "They need to get more basic skills in elementary school," Gary argued, "and there's too much television, too many sports, and too many after-school jobs."

# Knowing the Setting and Its History

Elementary teachers and their principals bristled. "They have the basic skills when they get to you! Just look at our test scores," Meg and Anne, the elementary principals, responded defensively. "We have so many subjects to prepare for, so little prep time, and we get the job done—the problem is in the high school," Elaine, one of the elementary teachers, added with a noticeable tone of exasperation. Cheryl, another elementary teacher, also blamed the curriculum and text. Later, in private, they all attributed the problems at the high school to poor teaching. The antipathy toward Gary and his point of view was so marked that I had to spend some time the following week personally reassuring some elementary teachers and principals that they were not being targeted for blame. The following is from a note that I attached to the minutes.

> I know that the discussion kindled some uncomfortable feelings. It may be important and useful for us to deal with these feelings as a professional group, because we certainly don't want them to go beyond us into the community.
> 
> Pride in our profession and in the efforts of our colleagues can only result in more receptive kids and respect from our parents. Let's deal with the misconceptions and misunderstandings so that we can go forward and be the best! A little conflict may go a long way to overcome nonproductive complacency.

Overlooked by all were everyone's expectations and lack of self-reflection. These were dealt with later when the emotional conflicts were replaced by more rational thought. This type of suspicion and blame shifting between teachers at different levels is not uncommon in education, and it may not be remedied by site-based management cultures. Collegial clusters of teachers across grade levels seems more encouraging.

Although preparation for the change in mathematics instruction began the same school year as the first collaborative building plans, and BLTs and the math needs assessment and planning teams involved some of the same people, the teams functionally existed as separate collegial clusters. One cluster focused on the curriculum and instruction in mathematics and the others on the more general aspects of school climate and culture. Not until the third year did some cohesion of the clusters begin, but interactive, supportive, and dragging effects were soon obvious. I will identify these as we proceed.

## Setting Goals or Standards: What Should Be?

Fortunately, cluster members agreed that there was a problem and that the general goals or outcomes for the district's students needed to be changed. The NCTM (1989b) standards had not yet been published, but the various national reports gave us some ideas about outcomes and helped by mitigating personal guilt. Because the problem was shared nationally, the needs assessment team members were encouraged as a collegial cluster to look beyond their own classrooms to other places and into the future. With the help of my prodding, we began to develop a consensual vision.

The goals we used as a basis for the needs assessment were temporary and open-ended: a general gathering of information about desired and accomplished objectives, existing conditions, possibilities, and opinions. They would be modified in the planning stage as we heard more voices and learned more. The final diagnosis of program needs and the rationale for change were based on the modified outcomes, which I will discuss in Chapter 6. In the first year of implementation, the subsequently published document of NCTM (1989b) standards broadened our team's vision and clarified, fortified, and enhanced our outcome goals with important additional specifics. Readers should also know that none of us were aware of much of the ongoing cognitive research in mathematics at this time. We still had a great deal to learn from others and from ourselves.

## The Formal Assessment: Documenting What Is

The next task of the needs assessment cluster was to document the gap between our developing vision and the state of our instructional program and to hear other voices. To do this, we had to decide on the form and subjects of our analyses and then design appropriate assessment instruments. Although there are currently strong prescriptions from varying levels to include parents, students, and other community members in educational goal setting, they were not involved in the original group. The cluster decided, however, to involve them as subjects in the assessment and in the implementation process. Working both in the large group and in smaller subcommittees, we developed a plan and the instruments to gather information from a variety of internal and external sources. It consisted of the following:

# Knowing the Setting and Its History

- An analysis of current student data (standardized and local test scores and course participation rates)
- A self-assessment of the most frequently used classroom instructional strategies by K-6 teachers
- A survey of coverage of New York State objectives with the written curriculum as a criterion by K-6 teachers (We also asked them if they would have addressed the objectives if they had the time.)
- A questionnaire survey of parents, high school students, and teachers
- Visitations by high school, middle school, and elementary teachers to see "What is?" in other districts
- An analysis of SAT student responses

## Learning From Data

After the data were collected and collated and visitations to other school districts were completed, reports on the findings were shared with the needs assessment cluster as a whole. We met again to consider its many implications. It was obvious, on the basis of the teachers' own perceptions, that the written New York State curriculum objectives were not all addressed at the elementary level. Only approximately 69% of the objectives were recognized as touched on by teachers, although 89% of them were rated as desirable. This did not measure accomplishment or account for a cumulative longitudinal effect through several grade levels. This finding about the discrepancy between written and taught objectives agrees with the findings of many other researchers (e.g., Barr, 1988; Glatthorn, 1987).

> The teacher is an active curriculum maker who, day by day, makes important decisions about what is taught and how it is taught; in making those decisions, the teacher responds to numerous pressures and influences. The written curriculum plays a varying role in influencing teacher decision making—but at best, it is only one of several factors that the teacher considers. (Glatthorn, 1987, p. 20)

At the elementary and middle school levels, a separate survey asked the teachers to assess the frequency with which they used the following instructional strategies: paper-and-pencil drill and practice, direct instruction without manipulatives or with manipulatives, independent practice with manipulatives, and individual coaching. The results indicated little use of manipulatives, even at the first-grade level. Although drill and practice was not the most highly ranked activity (for frequency of use) on the survey, this result may have been somewhat spurious because, as we learned in important follow-up interviews, some teachers may have not considered time spent by the children on drill and practice activities as an instructional strategy.[2] My observations indicated that in actual practice, the most math time was spent by the children at their seats in this endeavor. Individual coaching often accompanied the seat work but usually involved correction of errors rather than developmental interactions.[3] Direct whole-group teacher instruction without manipulatives was the most highly ranked strategy at every level except for kindergarten.

The high school teachers were particularly interested in the survey of 8th to 12th graders, parents of these students, and their teachers. Several questions were designed to explore expectations and confidence levels. Results indicated that although expectations on the part of the teachers, older students, and parents were better than predicted, they were still weak. Student confidence levels were poor and decreased with the students' age, but the teachers and parents were more pessimistic than the students. They believed that success in mathematics came only to those who were born with the appropriate talent and that working hard or being interested did not matter. They were not too different from others in this country. The international study by McNight et al. (1987) also found that American parents are less likely than Chinese and Japanese parents to attribute success in mathematics to effort expended (see also National Education Commission on Time and Learning, 1994).

The highest level of disagreement with the idea that a person needed to be born with math ability to succeed was expressed by younger students. This matched their somewhat higher confidence level. Were schools the cause of the damage to our older students' confidence? Were parents such as Jean Brown so complacent and stressed once they had made the sacrifices necessary to move into our district that they did little to encourage their kids to work hard and have lofty goals?

An interesting but predictable difference between parents and teachers was noted in the more positive response of parents to the

# Knowing the Setting and Its History

question that asked if they should encourage students to go beyond the required 2 years of math. Our teachers had always felt that they were the best judges of students' ability, and they resented pressure from parents to override their decisions. My experience was that some parents, unfortunately, were not willing to confront either their children or teachers when there was disagreement—they either didn't believe they could succeed or didn't care to persist.

Parents considered math more practical than either the teachers or the students—maybe because all that they remembered from their own experience was what they had used! Most revealing, but not unexpected, was a general continuous decrease of enjoyment of math classes by students from the 7th to the 12th grade. Combined with a lack of confidence and low adult expectations, this could easily have discouraged our students' participation and diminished their achievement in mathematics. Of course, the direction of the cause and effect relationship is not clear, and a history of failure to achieve could have depreciated enjoyment.[4]

The high school staff also looked at the testing data and Regents course participation rates with great frustration; they felt a decided lack of power in dealing with the problem. The Regents curriculum has little flexibility. It was packed tight, sometimes with topics the teachers felt were inappropriate or unnecessary. But there was little they could do. The state controlled the curriculum with its tests, and they were bound to it by a tradition of parent and community values and expectations. The analysis of SAT responses showed that South Vale students frequently missed questions that required just good number sense or estimation skills and that students were omitting questions at a much higher rate than students nationally. Was this because of lack of confidence or low expectations as indicated by the survey? Was it because the district didn't give the students enough time (other districts we visited had extended the time for some students)? Was it poor test-taking skills, or was something basically wrong with the way we taught mathematics? Wasn't there something we could do to improve this situation?

## Using What You Have Learned

Although each attempt at renewal is subject to the history and present culture of the particular situation, certain commonalities may be worth knowing and the solutions of others may be worth considering. Unquestionably common is the need to take the time to discover and understand the particular history and then perhaps to use it to make connections to new visions and voices. Together they may form a solid preparation stage for change. It may also be useful to compare the preparation stages of the two concurrent reform efforts I have previously described. And then, on the basis of previous knowledge and experience with change, readers may try to predict the relative effectiveness of the efforts. Reserve final judgment until you learn of the subsequent outcomes!

These factors marked the preparation for SBCDM:

- The source of the vision was external, unclear, and poorly communicated in a compressed period of time.
- The voices of powerful opinion leaders were engaged from the start, but little attention was paid to other voices.
- Leadership was inconsistent as leaders changed.
- The history had many traditions that needed to be overcome, especially those of roles and preserves of power.
- Data gathering about the present culture was closed-ended, externally designed, and squeezed into a short period of time.
- Some prestige and monetary rewards were attached to participation by teachers and other staff—none for administrators.

These factors marked the preparation for mathematics program reform:

- The vision came from an internal and recognizable source.
- Sizable effort and time were devoted to listening to other voices, modifying the vision in response, and transferring the vision to others.
- Leadership was consistent.
- Although the history revealed habits of practice, external power constraints, and anachronistic values that needed to be overcome, capacity to do this was lacking. Problems were recognized, but the blame was shifted to others.
- A variety of data from a wide range of sources was gathered in open-ended as well as in more definitive ways.

- There was no prestige or monetary reward for anyone in this preparatory period.

In a study in the late 1970s, I attempted to predict principals' "receptivity for change" by incorporating all of the climate of change predisposing factors then existent in the literature into a "receptivity index" (Solomon, 1977, p. 39). Neither the index nor any of the individual factors of which it was composed was a strong predictor, although "history of change" was promising. History, in this earlier study, was merely a comparative record of previously implemented innovations. Districts with more of these had principals who were more open to change. Perhaps experience and consequent knowledge of the variables of change made the respondent administrators in my research more confident and receptive; teachers may have responded differently. It was useful for me to be aware of the variables of change (those I have already explored and those in the chapters ahead). In the same study, however, I discovered that innovations that dealt directly with a changing teacher role were the least predictable either by the index or by the history element. The larger culture change of site-based decision making required new roles for teachers, principals, and others. These roles are associated with traditional preserves of power. Calls for reform that require significant changes in the distribution of power—even the power preserve of the classroom teacher over students—may underestimate the resistance of the established system (Sarason 1990, 1993).

Listening to the voices of the past and present through reflective peer interactions and documenting them with the research of an open-ended needs assessment are good preparation for change. It takes effective leadership to enable people to deal with history, especially as history is related to the preserves of power and control and the comforts of previous ownership. Leaders can also help people decide what is worthy of transmission and what needs to be transformed. The following chapter describes how a variety of existing, emerging, and changing leadership sources can direct or impede progress toward that end.

## Notes

1. The quotes from Jean Brown here and in other places in this book are a composite from interviews of parents conducted by my colleague Edward Westervelt (1993).

2. This was despite research evidence that most learning in traditional classes takes place inductively while the children work on problems. See Van Lehn (1986).

3. This compares with the Wisconsin findings of Peterson and Fennema (1985), who found that 47% of student math time was spent in seat work and 43% in whole-group instruction.

4. The National Assessment of Educational Progress found a similar decline in confidence and enjoyment. See Dossey et al. (1988).

# 4

# Leadership
## The Judicious Management of Power

### About This Chapter

This chapter begins an analysis of the critical variables of leadership and power as they affect the process of change. After defining the variables and explaining the relationship between them, I will provide some examples of the different sources and types of leadership that were manifested in the South Vale experience, focusing in each case on how power was managed. "Loosely coupled" (Weick, 1976, p. 1) organizations such as schools can be breeding grounds for emerging leaders, and collegial cultures nurture them—as long as there is a flexible flow of power.

In subsequent chapters, I will review how power translates into the actions of support and pressure that are necessary for transformation to new states and suggest how power is generated by increased capacity and constrained by time. Readers, however, need to remember that leadership is not just about managing power. Vision, listening to voices and history, and responding to them count as well.

### Defining Leadership and Power

A basic premise of the theory of entropy is that things have a natural tendency to move from an ordered state to a disordered state.

They run down. That is why housework never ends; people have to return things to order. That is also why schools are either improving or getting worse: Schools are never static; they are always changing. Improving them requires constant sources of new energy—the energy of effective leadership with power.

Leadership has been commonly defined in the literature with minor variation as "effective influence" (Argyris, 1976, p. 227) or as directing others toward achievement of goals. If leaders influence others, they are then effective leaders. Zalesnick (cited in Reitzug, 1994) has added the qualification that "leadership inevitably requires using power to influence the thoughts and actions of others" (p. 284).

Power, which may be the broader concept, has been defined as "the basic energy to initiate and sustain action, translating intention into reality; the quality without which leaders can not lead" (Bennis & Nanus, 1985, p. 17). Power gets things started and keeps them going. Although power itself has also been defined as the ability to control or influence others, I add the ability to control one's self and the environment to that definition. In all cases, power implies the potential for control and for using or releasing energy.

A common conception about power and the ability to influence others is that power is connected to the ability to dispense tangible rewards and punishments. But that concept may be too limiting unless one stretches the concept to the intangible satisfaction of complex human needs. A crying infant has power over his or her parents, and the reward may be cessation of the crying. But the helpless infant has power over the parents just in their need to nurture, and the school-age child has power over the teacher because of the teacher's imperative to reach the student. The teacher, in turn, gains a sense of power when successful at this task. Just having power, however, is a passive or potential energy state. Although power may provide a feeling of satisfaction, it does not get things done until it is used or given away and has had response.

When power is used to influence others (rather than one's self or the environment) to do something, it connects to leadership. In combination then, I can define *leadership* as the active and directed use of power to influence others. Can effective leadership exist without power? I think not, but the power need not come from nominal authority or be accompanied by the ability to bestow tangible rewards or punishments. Charismatic individuals can influence

# Leadership: The Judicious Management of Power

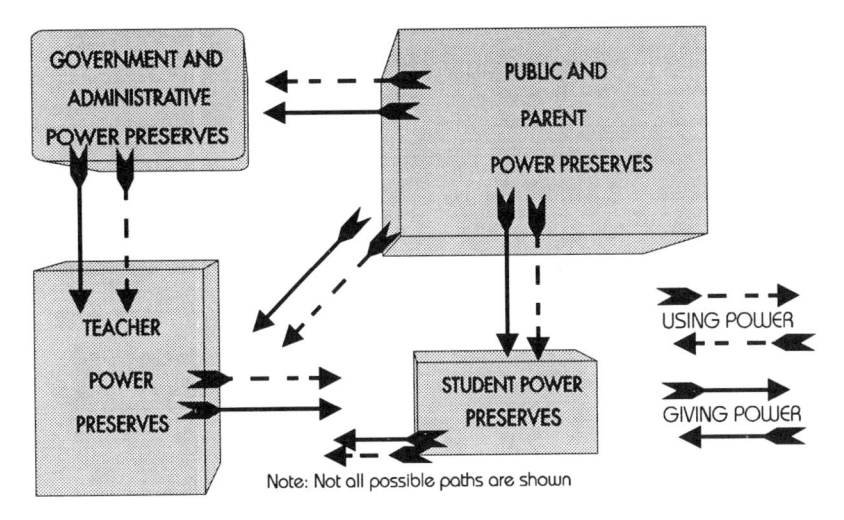

**Figure 4.1.** The Transfer of Power

others without such accoutrements. They can even influence others by giving them power or by helping them build it for themselves.

I believe, as do many others (e.g., Bennis & Nanus, 1985), that effective leaders manage power well, using their own preserves of power for direct control when needed or giving it to others as an indirect method of effective influence. When an administrator gives teachers voice by letting them decide what the curriculum should be, the administrator may be losing some control to the teachers. But if having that control increases the teachers' capacity to enable students to learn, then in the long run the administrator-leader has influenced others and, in effect, regained power from the teachers.

As I described in Chapter 2, my power as a principal was greatly increased by my professional growth committee and by the support of my staff. Parents give power to the schools when they entrust them with their children's education. They may also use their power to influence what happens there. Teachers use their power to control their students and counteract the power that students have over them, but teachers also give power to students as they increase their capacity to control themselves, others, and their environment. Students, in their peer interactions, both use and give each other power (in its exaggerated form, the power of street gangs).

Figure 4.1 illustrates the multidirectional possibilities of the transfer of power as it relates to public education. This consolidated diagram does not show every path in detail. For example, the administrative power preserve in the diagram represents a hierarchy of administrative possibilities from principals to superintendents, to boards of education, and to state and federal governments. The public power preserve represents parents as well as other influential nongovernmental publics such as PTAs. The teacher power preserve represents individual teachers as well as their peer groups, site-based management teams, unions, and professional groups. The student power preserve includes the students and their peer groups.

Leadership power derives from many sources other than administrators. It can come from individuals and groups, both within and from outside the immediate culture. Neither the possession of power nor effective leadership guarantees a positive effect for schools. Leadership must be directed toward a set of goals that the teachers, parents, and students have determined to be their consensual vision for the good of the system. As we began to realize new goals for our schools in South Vale, leadership arrived from different sources and in response to different needs. It was not all positive or directed toward our goals, but it was effective and presented itself in patterns worth noting.

## Developing Teacher-Leaders: Alan

Some of those actively involved on BLTs had an unprecedented and unpredicted opportunity for personal growth and leadership development. Alan, a highly intelligent high school mathematics teacher, a good mathematician, and an excellent communicator, is one example. Despite these attributes, before he became involved in SBCDM, his reputation as a teacher among parents and administrators and probably among his peers had not been particularly strong. Alan had a flourishing successful business on the side that gave him the personal rewards he wanted. As a matter of fact, he and I had previously disagreed about his professionalism when he had a part-time assignment at the middle school of which I was principal. I didn't think he cared enough about his teaching: He had some strong feelings about what was contractually required.

Alan became involved in the BLT and then on the DLT. His eloquence, leadership ability, and business experience gained him a new level of respect from everyone. He played a major role in creating the building improvement plans and in presenting them to the high school staff and was actively involved in the selection of the new high school principal and other staff members—a critical task for a BLT to overcome inconsistency of leadership. Alan then helped the new principal make the transition to a site-based management environment. When the district was asked to make a presentation at a statewide conference, he was the natural choice for spokesperson.

Meanwhile, Alan's attitude toward his teaching responsibilities changed as well. He helped his departmental colleagues accept the BLT goal of higher expectations and eruditely contributed to team meetings. Alan also began to spend more time preparing lessons, working with students after school, and calling parents. In a written goal statement for the formal evaluation process, he was the first teacher to set a goal for himself of test-measured increased performance by his students—an acceptance of responsibility by a teacher that did not totally project students' lack of achievement on to their own deficiencies. Alan's commitment to higher expectations showed in his resistance to allowing students to drop his Regents courses or transfer to lower-level alternatives. He used his power to resist their requests; then as he worked with them, in effect, he gave students their own new power of enlarged capacity.

I responded to this change in attitude by suggesting that he consider the challenge of upper-level courses, which he enthusiastically accepted and at which he soon became expert in building his own capacity and adding to his power over self and his environment. Alan is a good example of how involvement in collaborative management can serve an individual's needs and, as a consequence, increase job satisfaction and performance. His need for power and control was now met through his involvement in the collaborative management process. His capacity as a teacher and teacher-leader was now free to grow as the resistance to administrator-applied power was diffused in a collegial relationship, and he had a new personal reality of his professional responsibilities and potential. The change in Alan represents the pattern of giving power to others to influence them. His ability to influence others represents the pattern of the potential power of teacher-leaders.

## The Conflicting Visions of New Leaders: Jim

Our original district improvement plan had been developed under the leadership of Peter, who had risen quickly from his position as assistant principal to curriculum director for communication arts and then to assistant to the superintendent. Peter was young and charismatic. He had a natural, unassuming, and comfortable manner with staff members; they both admired and liked him. He was involved in the effort to improve our program from the start and understood the connection between the effective schools criteria and the plan to use site-based management as a vehicle for achieving them. This understanding was not shared by many of the staff, but they trusted Peter. Unfortunately, after the first year of implementation, Peter left and was replaced by Jim, who was completely new to the district.

By that time, the district also had two new principals who had not been there at the beginning. A third new one came the year after Jim took over as assistant superintendent. Jim was much more remote and serious in his interpersonal relationships. Like most newcomers, he was anxious to make an impression. During his first year, he formed several new committees—completely separate from the BLTs (site-based teams). The effective strategies committee was formed to research and share effective classroom strategies. The staff development committee was separately constituted to plan formal in-service programs and conference day plans. Teachers volunteered for these, but administrators were expected to be on both committees. Although some overlap of people occurred, a great deal of time was spent at these committee meetings and at BLT meetings informing each other of the various activities and decisions.

The principals felt particularly imposed on by the many meetings. They wanted to help Jim, but they were busy with their own building teams and other responsibilities. "I've heard this three times already and I have to get back to my building," was Meg's (an elementary principal) legitimate complaint. Taking Meg away from her building deprived her of time and power. The other curriculum director and I were also overinvolved but felt the need to protect curriculum interests.

Jim was also unfamiliar with our curriculum cycle. When he pressured the staff development committee for a variety of programs in which he was personally interested, we saw a conflict with our own needs. He had not been there for the mathematics needs assessment and did not immediately see in-service in that area as a priority. We finally worked out a compromise, but I was uncomfortable with the competition for the teachers' time and with the resulting delay of our formal in-service program.

# Leadership: The Judicious Management of Power

Propitiously, one of the programs that Jim brought to the district because he had used it in his previous position proved to be quite helpful. The Teacher Expectations and Student Achievement (TESA) program translates research into classroom practices that communicate higher expectations to students. The program has enjoyed significant success and widespread implementation (Kerman, 1979). TESA was supportive of the high school goal of higher expectations, and its peer coaching component was a model for our future method for maintaining change, which uses experienced teachers to mentor novices (see Chapter 8).

Meanwhile, Jim was neither welcomed nor comfortable at the site-based team meetings. The teachers felt that he was not committed to their agendas or to the concept of shared management. Because Jim's experience had been only at the high school level, the elementary school teachers saw him as an uninformed outsider. Jim's tenacity in his own vision made him seem rigid and insensitive to their voices. After one meeting, Elaine, the teacher I will describe later, expressed her frustration: "He just doesn't listen." The teachers were offering only indirect messages. As I discussed in Chapter 2, these were not heeded.

The principals, new to site-based management and, in two instances, new in their jobs, were unsure of their own power status and equally uncomfortable about giving some away. Fortunately, the building teams had gathered some momentum and were proceeding with their plans. They pressured their colleagues on the staff development committee to plan in-service programs that would increase their capacity to manage and come to consensus. Jim eventually responded to the BLT needs and arranged for in-service programs in stress management and group dynamics—but not until his own agenda had been completed.

Jim had made the same mistake that many new administrators make (I did it, too, in my first year as principal). Anxious to act on well-intentioned personal visions and insecure in their ability to influence others in more subtle ways, they lunge ahead and use the nominal power of authority to effect change. Like Jim, they tend to ignore or underestimate the power and needs of the existing culture and its history. They do little to support the previous consensus of goals and deprive those over whom they have power the resources needed to accomplish them. Because they are nominal leaders, little direct protest occurs, just silent acquiescence or inaudible indirect messages.

An understanding of the limitations of the human energy resources in the culture is critical for the effective leader of change. At South Vale, we were all busy with this tremendous agenda of reform. Meg and her teachers needed time in their building, and I needed them and their time as well, but our complaints were whispered to each other. In their review of the research on teacher commitment, Firestone and Pennell (1993) also point out that teachers resent the time that meetings take away from the source of their greatest satisfaction: their classroom work.

Time is a limiting resource for the energies of overworked staffs and a variable of change that I will address more comprehensively in Chapter 8. Distribution of tasks among a variety of collegial clusters can ease the time and energy drain of new decision making and professional growth responsibilities for teachers and administrators and may prevent burnout. But needed also is articulation between the clusters to avoid duplication of human effort and to assure consensus of voices and coherence of vision (see Chapters 7 and 8). Jim would have been better off waiting for a bit while absorbing and being absorbed into the ambient culture and getting a better picture of the available resources. He might have found a way to accomplish his vision through the struggling, but viable, system of SBCDM. And perhaps, as he grew more secure, he might have been able to strengthen the system and influence others by giving them some of his power.

In Chapter 1, I discussed the variables of change and noted that capacity building, pressure, and support were in the action path of changes in reflective practice. These variables need to be initiated by the leadership sources of power. Continued action requires constant energy. The battery gets the motor started, but getting anywhere requires a steady supply of new energy-releasing gasoline. Although his intent was sincere, Jim did not supply the fuel of support and capacity building as it was needed. Jim represents the problem pattern of changing leaders, inadequately involved or informed of a system's history, whose effective power is not directed toward its consensual vision. This pattern is often associated with the use of power for control rather than with the giving of power to generate influence.

## Developing Principal Leaders: Anne

When Anne first arrived at Park Lane School as a new principal, she made some of the same mistakes as Jim. She was quite young,

## Leadership: The Judicious Management of Power

came straight out of a kindergarten classroom, and was a sharp contrast to the previous principal, Ted. Anne was highly structured and organized. Her leadership approach was definitively task oriented. Ted, equally young and attractive, had relied substantially on his charming personality and helpful consideration to get things done. Ted was always there when someone had a problem with a movie projector or some science experiment, but the atmosphere was quite relaxed. He had run what most people might call a "loose shop."

One of Anne's first unwelcome decisions had been to lock up the supply storeroom. Her style was to establish a clear structure, conduct carefully planned meetings, issue memos and newsletters, and, in general, get things organized. She used her power in a traditional way and was too insecure to give it away. Her staff complained that she was not as visible in the halls and classrooms as they would have preferred. Anne's presence outside of her office more would have given the staff some of the support they were used to and would have compensated for her being less likely to engage easily in the lunchroom banter at which Ted excelled. This repartee had served Ted well. It gave him a line of communication that enabled him to perceive and sometimes defuse incipient staff problems. He was not particularly liked by parents, who felt that a tighter rein on what was happening in the school would be better. Anne provided this, but her approach was not appreciated by the staff, who saw her decisions as arbitrary—even oppressive.

The staff at Park Lane was younger than the staff at the other elementary school. It was sparked by a group of especially energetic and outspoken young teachers, including Elaine and most of the elementary special education teachers. Uncomfortable with Anne's leadership style, they welcomed the opportunity for site-based management, and I was surprised that they did not identify leadership as a problem in the original needs assessment. The BLT chose other improvements as first-year priorities but looked forward to having more control over Anne's edicts.

Fortunately, Anne maintained her cool, and the hope of finding cooperative solutions to their problems prevailed throughout the first planning stage. After some soul-searching preliminary meetings, the BLT at Park Lane began to find some common ground. The teachers had a formal forum and process for sharing their grievances, and Anne, who preferred this more directed environment to the lunchroom repartee, began to listen. Faced with their new responsibilities for planning and decision making, the staff appreciated Anne's organizational abilities. She listened to them and learned that they had some pretty good ideas about what would work and what wouldn't.

As she became more comfortable with her role, Anne began to loosen up. She was one of the original school improvement planners and the only tenured principal for the first few years. She was comfortable enough to see collaborative site-based management as a way to improve both her school and her relationship with staff. As the Park Lane BLT grew stronger, the school flourished. They received many rewards and national recognition as an outstanding school—and everyone gained power.

Anne represents the pattern of a nominal leader who discovered that she could gain power and achieve success by giving some control to others. Like many of us, as time passed and the context changed, Anne took some backward steps, but that is a different story. I will come back to it in Chapter 8.

## Giving Voice to Teacher-Leaders: Elaine

When the original math needs assessment group (described in Chapter 3) was disbanded, we formed three new planning clusters. The elementary cluster met for a week during the ensuing summer. For the first time, there was some monetary compensation for the time spent. Several of the original needs assessors now participated as planners, and additional elementary teachers joined to form a mixed and representative group. A majority of the members were from Park Lane School, but at least one representative for each grade, K-3, was from the other school. With one exception, they were experienced teachers, although their ages varied; the two special education teachers in the group were the youngest. Almost everyone had worked with others in the group before and also had worked closely with me. In my previous role as district science coordinator, I had a long-term experience implementing a science program with the older group. Elaine, one of the younger teachers, had been on the middle school staff when I was principal. Despite her youth, she quickly emerged as the group's significant teacher-leader.

Elaine had lived in South Vale while growing up and had attended our schools. She had a high energy level: Her classroom was always buzzing with creative and highly organized activity. Children in her classes were never bored, and they were secure because they always knew what to expect from her—so did I. Elaine had started out as a special education teacher. Her patience and enthusiasm had made her successful with her challenging special students, but her restless and change-seeking personality had motivated her to try teaching the regular classes. Elaine's assignment to a regular third-grade class was therefore relatively new and stimulating, and she was already tuned in to dealing with individual differences in children. Her more recent training in special education also made her more knowledgeable and receptive to constructivist ideas.

A strong, free, and animated spirit, Elaine was admired by her colleagues. She was not easily intimidated by either their peer influence or the pressure of administrators and parents. She spoke her mind easily, with deserved confidence, and was the spark who set a positive tone for the others. She asked perceptive questions in our reflections, encouraged her colleagues, and was like a child at Christmas as she breathlessly perused catalogs for manipulative materials. "I can't wait to try these with the children," she squealed, and the others caught her enthusiasm. It was soon obvious that Elaine's leadership would have an important impact on the group's chances for success.

As a whole, the elementary planning cluster members would have been judged by their colleagues, administrators, and parents as strong teachers but not necessarily as the 10 best. They were, as individuals, respected by their colleagues. They were not, however, at this point ready to use power to influence others. After a week of reflection on the data and their own experience and knowledge and after listening intently to the guests I invited for one afternoon, they decided to pilot a program of change limited to their own group. Although I suggested that they experiment with some different programs that we had learned about in our visits and from our guests, they all decided on the same text that had a developmental approach and good supporting materials. Making your own decision and being different requires taking a risk! Teachers need the comfort of collegial groups.

Their willingness, as a group, to take a risk was coupled with a sense of *ownership* for the decisions they made. This helped to muddle through the difficulties with little anxiety during the first year. They soon became a well-defined collegial cluster, engaged and reflective as they took ownership of the mathematics curriculum change; their power increased as they gained capacity, and then they became leaders! As I will describe in the chapters ahead, this cluster provided a nucleus of support in the future stages of implementation and maintenance; they shared their power by helping others gain capacity.

Elaine and her colleagues represent the pattern of emerging teacher-leadership that forms when power and trust are shared. Sustaining such leadership requires the continuing support of those who already have power until teachers' capacity grows and increases their power to the necessary level. If responsibility for the wise use of this power is then assumed by teachers, it will be self-perpetuating. Readers will see some of this happening in subsequent discussions of capacity.

### Protecting Power Preserves: Greta

Not all leaders will be productive in the process of change. Each system component has its own power preserve, and change—especially change that tinkers with traditional roles or comforts—threatens the loss of power. Greta presents an example of a teacher-leader with the power to resist change.

Greta, an experienced fourth-grade teacher, was highly organized and always in control. I had gotten to know Greta fairly well in my previous roles as teacher, district science coordinator, and principal. Like many of the older staff, both of us lived in the community; her children attended our schools. Although Greta was close to retirement age when our school management and math program change began, she had a bouncy manner and a high energy level. When she visited the middle school with her class for orientation while I was principal, she always made a special effort to seek me out and tell me in a concerned manner about her students' problems and then proudly detail how she had handled them. This nurturing approach and her strong classroom discipline impressed the parents. They often requested that the principal assign Greta as their children's teacher.

Consequently, Greta seemed quite secure in her role. Her self-assured manner and outspokenness gained her much respect from her peers. She was an informal leader. In casual peer interactions (especially at lunch), she was sometimes critical, as were others, of

# Leadership: The Judicious Management of Power

administrative actions, but her willingness to complain openly at faculty meetings was not too common among elementary teachers. I found this forthright communication with administrators to be helpful, although aggravating, because it enabled me to tune in on teachers' needs and anxieties. In private, however, Greta seemed anxious to gain approval. One day, she showed me her plan book and proudly declared, "I teach math and science every day. Not everyone does."

Greta's class always appeared to be on task and polite. I had never seen her actually engaged in group discourse with the children—it seemed as though she immediately cut it off when I entered the room. Usually, children were at her desk having written work corrected while others were busily engaged in completing theirs. When I first asked if she was using manipulatives, she replied, "I don't have time to use the manipulatives because the book will never be finished if I do. What will the parents say when no ditto sheets come home?"

Conscientious teachers are usually concerned with covering the curriculum. In most cases, this is related to using a text or workbook, but often it is influenced by teacher beliefs and their anxiety over abandoning familiar or apparently successful practices (see e.g., Barr, 1988; Porter, Floden, Freeman, Schmidt, & Schwille, 1988). Covering a text or workbook brings an easily measured "psychic reward" (Lortie, 1975, p. 101). It is also proof to others that a teacher has done a good job. Some parents did complain as we implemented our changes, and we dealt with their concerns by including them in the reeducation process (see Chapter 7). Greta's teacher imperative, however, was to make sure that every blank space in the workbook was filled and that every line from a prescribed text was read, assigned, and perhaps discussed. This was more important than using the manipulatives I found in unopened packages in her classroom.

Early in the second year, when implementation of the mathematics program became districtwide, Meg, Greta's principal, had to monitor the copy machine to prevent her and other anxious teachers from copying the pages of drill and practice from the old mathematics workbooks. This occurred despite evidence from colleagues, who had piloted the new program, that students learned just as well when they constructed their own understandings with a few meaningful experiences. Some worried teachers also surreptitiously administered the suspended computation part of a standardized test to reassure themselves that their kids were up to par.

## Power in the Classroom

Attempts to transfer ownership of new practices to teachers are often tied up in their own struggle for power. Teachers are the leaders in their classes and have power over their students. They have already selected those classroom practices that give them comfort, satisfaction, and control. In the previous specific example, anxiety over loss of control of students proved to be a strong constraining factor in the willingness of teachers to shift toward the use of manipulatives and away from ditto-sheet-managed seat work. They had used the seat work to control their students.

In an interview with beginning teachers who had experienced teachers as mentors, Sarason (1990) discovered that they were told that "establishing (in the classroom) the authority and power of the teacher were absolutely essential." The source of great stress in that beginning time was that they often found themselves "on the brink of doing things that were psychologically wrong" and their fear was that "their inadequacies would come to the attention of the principal and other teachers—that is those who had the power and influence to devalue them" (p. 79).

In a reflection on her mentoring role with new teachers, Elaine made the following observations about one of her mentorees.

> Don has classroom management problems. He needs to get his children to focus in. He takes my telling this very well because he knows that eventually the principal will be in to observe, and I've told him he needs to control the kids better! Once he gets this control and they focus, his lessons will be more successful. Also he seems to think that once all the children are engaged in an activity he can sit at his desk and work on something else. He has to work with the kids all the time! Being with me and April [another experienced teacher with whom Elaine worked closely] must be difficult for him, too, because I sense he thinks teaching is easy. (see Chapter 1, note 3)

When Meg and I asked Greta to abandon a familiar practice, we asked her to give up something over which she had control, a practice that allowed her to maintain control over her students. We exerted influence, diminishing her power of free choice—and she felt threatened. The principals also felt threatened when they realized that

# Leadership: The Judicious Management of Power

collaborative, site-based management meant giving up some of their traditional decision-making prerogatives. Anxious individuals who are concerned about losing power can quickly grow into systemwide constraints to the processes of change. These constraints are not commonly active and vocal; mostly they are in the form of passive resistance to change.

Education cannot afford the lack of accountability and undependability of classroom autonomy any more. Even the most revered professions have group standards (Darling-Hammond, 1988). But teachers need the opportunity as collegial groups or clusters to set those standards—not politicians! Teachers in their collegial clusters, however, will have to be in a two-way interactive discourse with other shareholders: parents, students, and the community at large. They must listen and respond to the rapidly changing societal needs and values while reassuring those who question the efficacy of their efforts. They can no longer remain bounded in their classrooms, their buildings, or other pedagogical entities.

Principals, meanwhile, may need to sacrifice some of the "power" that was traditionally theirs, perhaps in exchange for collegial pressure to encourage reflection and productive change and, ultimately, for collegial willingness to take responsibility for some of what may not have really been under their *true* control: the everyday instruction behind the closed doors of the classroom. The limited classroom observations of the past were rarely fruitful, especially with experienced teachers (Wise & Darling-Hammond, 1984).

## Sharing Responsibility and Power

The sacrifice of power does not mean absolution from responsibility. Nominal leaders must share power and responsibility as well. I was disappointed that not one of the building principals participated in the mathematics planning group or in the formal in-service course. They, of course, were highly involved in the site-based management reform and were relieved to have the math out of their hands. They relied on me. My history as a building principal made them more trusting and power giving and made me more tolerant of their peripheral involvement. My responsibility for management of the budget also left them formally out of the material resource allocation responsibility. Although they countersigned budgets, they made only a few specific decisions about what to buy, which I always honored.

The control of money brings power. This arrangement had always set up some competition for control between the curriculum directors and the building principals. The locus of power actually varied during the almost 25-year time span of this organization, depending on the tenure of changing individuals. New administrators in either role were intimidated by more secure individuals in the other role. Elementary teachers and principals were less likely to accept the direct supervision of the curriculum people than secondary teachers, who were more subject oriented.

This is not to eschew the principals' support. They made their support clear to everyone in a number of ways, such as providing teaching assistants for piloting teachers, monitoring the use of the copy machine for the disfavored drill and practice activities, and helping me schedule the variety of workshops and meetings. They even consulted with me after observing teachers to check their perceptions of what was right or wrong in the lessons. Their personal yearly management plans also included objectives that addressed our cooperative efforts. Their support was open and consistent, and the program would not have succeeded without it.

Sharing of power worked in this case, but giving away some power should not imply complete abdication from responsibility. Some presence in the training program would have firmed up the principals' leadership commitment, given them the new capacity to facilitate the growth of teachers' capacity, and, most important, mitigated any future interruption in evocator leadership. Consistency of leadership is a decided variable in the change process. Fortunately, I was able to stay with the task for a long enough time—until the teachers took over. This is not always the case. The backup power of a team of educated and committed administrators is a fail-safe necessity unless a strong collegial culture can take up the slack. Such a team developed at Park Lane School, but, unfortunately, the support energy has not sustained it.

## Other Power Sources

The change to site-based management has been predicted as more difficult at the high school level. The experience at South Vale,

## Leadership: The Judicious Management of Power

however, demonstrated that little difference existed initially in the strength of the developing collegial culture of the high school and elementary BLTs. In fact, the high school BLT continues to attract capable and experienced teachers and is a continuing source for district teacher leadership.

During a longer time span, however, differences appeared between the levels in the direction of BLT efforts. In contrast to the gradual shift toward more curricular concerns by the middle school and elementary BLTs, the high school building team remained concentrated on school climate, relegating curriculum and instructional considerations to the strongly bound departmental clusters. For example, little schoolwide attention was paid to the math teachers' decision to eliminate tracking.

The position of the high school as the element from which a student exits the common public school sequence also places it more squarely under the scrutiny and power preserves of the public and government. The reputation of a school district hinges disproportionately on the reputation of its high school. Parents worry about competition for college and jobs and are wary of departures from traditional norms. They and their organizations pressure legislators for state and federal controls and standards.

The complexity of the high school in its charge to meet both the many needs of adolescents and these externally imposed standards also adds to the problem. High school schedules that maximize the diversity of opportunity by offering a wide range of courses can be limiting and inflexible to varying individual needs because of the difficulty in fitting it all in. As has been proven in several other places, real innovation at this level requires a departure from the traditional American high school schedule (e.g., National Education Commission on Time and Learning, 1994; Sizer, 1984). Scheduling is a controlling but formidable task, not one that teachers are willing to undertake without special compensation. Significant innovations in scheduling are also hampered by union contracts that structure the teacher's day. As long as little recognition exists for the outside-of-classroom tasks that teachers must perform and no real shift in how schools are managed occurs, teachers will be reluctant to let go of their organizational power.

As I will describe in the following chapter, the South Vale high school teachers were without the power to change the high school Regents curriculum, which the community valued. They could not influence the high school principal to change the schedule to allow students additional time for more challenging courses. He was not ready to relinquish the power and control that responsibility for this task gave him, and central administration did not allocate the funds to make it an acceptable responsibility for teachers. Even if the principal had offered scheduling power to the high school building team, they probably would not have tackled it. They were already overworked and did not have the necessary energy reserve, confidence, and trust of their colleagues.

This minimization of power and trust, which is executed by the external controls of government and community and by the internal ones of high school traditions, does not increase teachers' capacity. To the contrary, it gives them an excuse for tracking students and for not being accountable. (I will address accountability and the power of tests more comprehensively in Chapter 7.) Most governmental mandates take power away from teachers. This is felt most strongly at the high school level, where it hinders the building of capacity of teachers and students. Only a glimmer of hope lies in the mandates that require participation in governance by teachers and parents because that participation is forced and requires the expenditure of already limited energy resources.

Unfortunately, the continuing content-centered focus of high school curriculum also perpetuates isolation and maintains traditional preserves of power. Teachers will not attain real control of the high school until their principals share their power over the schedule. Real restructuring of the content-isolated delivery of high school instruction will not occur until strong building teams, who see the advantages, break the norms and patterns of departmental power. Perhaps only the energy of interdisciplinary building teams, who generate authentic interdisciplinary assessments that are based on locally determined curriculum standards, can change this pattern (see Chapter 7). Departmental peer groups will have to learn to trust their colleagues, and governments and communities will have to trust the teachers, the parents, and their leaders. All will need to share responsibility and power.

## The Sources of Leadership and Transfer of Power

Bennis and Nanus (1985) have called power the currency of leaders. Like money, it can be traded, given away, and used for

# Leadership: The Judicious Management of Power

control, but it is useless when it sits under a mattress. A wise leader puts power into circulation! In a collegial culture in which power transfers easily and is given to others as frequently as it is used to control others, leadership for productive transformation can come from many sources. As Fullan (1990) has noted, "the driving force for change can initially come from inside or outside the school and from a variety of different roles. Once the model is fully functioning, leadership does indeed come from multiple sources simultaneously" (p. 21). The more the merrier, as long as there is consensus on the vision. Inconsistent leadership that pays little attention to the existing consensual vision or makes no attempt to develop a new consensus has less promise for making improvements. People will always be reluctant to give up power. Leaders have to deal with this as well as with the conflicting visions of other leadership sources. The following chapter will explore in greater detail how leaders, who are evocators of change, manage their power with pressure and support.

# 5

# Evoking Change With Support and Pressure

### About This Chapter

In Chapter 4, I discussed the sources of leadership and its incumbent attachment of power. Possession of power, however, does not predicate its use in the process of implementing productive change or in the realization of visions. Power can be used to maintain the status quo and, in some cases, to impede change or negate another's vision in favor of one's own. In this chapter, I will suggest how power can be used or given to provide the energy-requiring and controlling actions of support and pressure, which are needed for transformation to a desired new state. I will then describe how the passive failure to provide support is also controlling when it creates a stalemate or, perhaps, regression. The following chapters will provide examples of support actions that increase capacity and bring it to the point at which, with a minimum of support, a new state is self-sustaining.

### Defining Support and Pressure

Visions of systemic school reform require support for the people who must change to manifest that vision, but they also may require pressure on those who resist that change. As Huberman and Miles (1984) have stated, a well-balanced combination of pressure and support is usually necessary. Support as a variable of change has traditionally been linked with its complement pressure. More recently, however, as mentioned in Chapter 1, Huberman and Miles (1986) use the combination terms "supported enforcement" and "assistance" (p. 72).

I understand their reason for doing this, but because these variables differ in the way power is managed, it may be preferable for the purpose of definition to separate them. A supporting leader gives power to others. Many of the actions of supporting leaders, however, are the same as the actions of pressuring leaders. Pressure may be viewed as the countervailing variable to support only in that a pressuring leader uses power for control instead of giving it. A pressuring leader expends energy and takes some power away from others, but may, with complementary supporting actions, indirectly give away some power as well. Figure 5.1 illustrates the divergent actions of the variables and lists some examples of the overlapping or common actions.

Reitzug (1994) identifies support as one of three categories of empowering (or power-giving) principal behavior. His deconstruction of this behavior is useful, but for history's sake, I prefer to have the more general term *support* subsume what he calls *facilitation* and *possibility*. In his support category, Reitzug includes, for example, the power-giving support actions of "providing autonomy with responsibility for supporting practice, communicating trust, providing opportunities for conversation with others" (which I call peer reflections), and "honoring teachers' opinions" (p. 291). In his category of facilitation, he includes the overlapping pressure and support actions of "asking questions, wandering around," and "providing staff development activities" (p. 291). In his possibility category are the overlapping actions of providing tangible and intangible resources such as time and energy.

A pressuring leader will probably not employ the power-giving actions of Reitzug's support category but may use many actions from the facilitating and possibility categories. I will make additions such as modeling to Reitzug's list and illustrate them in examples below and in the following chapters. An important point to consider here is that a supporting leader expends his or her own energy resources and gives power to others—it goes into circulation.

# Evoking Change With Support and Pressure

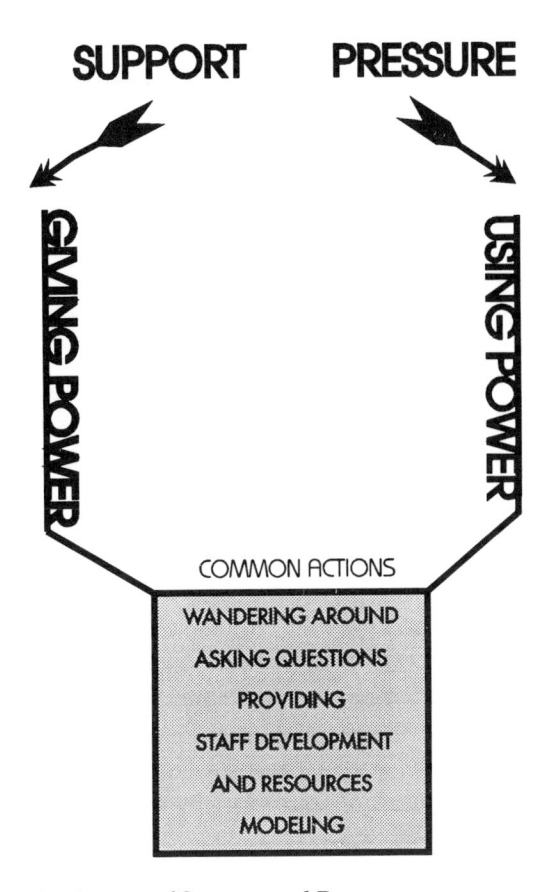

**Figure 5.1.** The Actions of Support and Pressure

## The Evocator and Prodding

If serious improvement of schools is to occur, people must change. But the "paradox of prodding" is that although real change is self-initiated, this rarely happens without prodding from an external leadership source (Hansen, 1967, p. 24). The leader who has traditionally been a prodder or evocator of change has been a visionary administrator, university professor, public figure, or government official issuing a mandate. I hope that in a restructured school, the evocator may also be a teacher-leader responding to internal collegial reflection on present practice (Lieberman & Miller, 1986). It is my experience that without strength in the role of the evocator, who must call forth the change, change will rarely occur.

As curriculum director, I was the evocator in the case of the district's mathematics reform, firmly supported by my superintendent, by the timeliness of the context, and by a team of teachers and principals. My long history in the school district and the tradition of power in the director's role were definite advantages in generating the necessary evocator actions in the mathematics program changes. Consistency without rigidity in that role was critical to success.

No counterpart leader guided the district through the reforms toward SBCDM. The turnover in district management deprived us of an evocator with strength. The superintendent never seemed too committed or involved and soon was preparing for his own departure. Within the first 3 years, the board of education had changed; the assistant superintendent in charge had changed twice; and the middle school, the high school, and one elementary school had new principals. All were struggling with their own capacities and feelings of security. School administrators tend to lead peripatetic lives. They come and go, rarely becoming mature and secure enough in a place to be comfortable with sharing and giving power to others.

Prodding requires the leader-evocator to manage power—either to use it or to give it to others. Tension over the possession of power seems to be an overwhelming characteristic of human civilizations. Although often painful or even devastating, this has not deterred humans from progress. Understanding power as a variable and building that understanding into planning for change may make the process and the future more promising. A shift in power is always attached to the change process, and no one likes to lose power. But sometimes the best way to prod is to give away some power in the form of support. It may be a necessary gift to those who must endure the discomfort of change. At other times, power must be used in the form of pressure. Secure people with clear and consistent visions manage power best. Administrators in new positions, dealing with unclear visions not their own with little direction from above, cannot be secure, especially when their traditional roles are threatened. At South Vale, the progress toward greater site-based decision making was hampered by inconsistent leadership and poor management of power.

Sarason (1993) cautions that administrators are poorly prepared. My own training in administration alerted me to the nature of power and its historical use, but it did not prepare me for the situation-bound decisions I would need to make, particularly those that required me to choose between the different power components of pressure and support. When I was an insecure novice, my more impatient inclination—although I always sensed cognitively that it was the wrong way to go—was to use my power to pressure others, rather than to give some power away and bide my time with support.

Although support, in its many forms, is the safest choice for the evocator, sometimes pressure is necessary. Each situation is unique. Quite frequently, evocators make mistakes. There are patterns, however, and knowing about them may improve chances for success. Readers may recognize these patterns from the situations I will now describe.

## The High School Mathematics Department

Like Gary, whom readers encountered in Chapter 3, most of the faculty of the high school mathematics department in South Vale were rather typical of secondary teachers. They were, as a whole, good mathematicians, independent, mature and well educated. Their attitude, however, was elitist, and they also had reputations as resistant to supervision. For more than 20 years, department members had been the source of teacher union leadership. Jill was the current long-term president, and George was the former long-term president. Alan, who was described in Chapter 4, was also involved with the teachers' union, but as the BLT chairperson, he was beginning to use a new venue as an opinion leader.

At the beginning, department teachers were not too thrilled with me as their curriculum director. The role of director was much too broad to have a close identity with one tightly-bound high school department. The teachers would have preferred a department chairperson, preferably from their own ranks and certainly one who had been a math teacher, not a science teacher and principal such as me. I needed to gain credibility with this group and listen carefully to the voices of its members.

Early in the first year, I asked George (who was the most senior and secure of the group) if I could sit in on his advanced classes to refresh my knowledge of the subject matter. I helped get the budget allocations that department teachers wanted and supported them whenever possible with parents, students, and the high school principal. Except for Gary, however, they had not attended any of the mathematics needs assessment team meetings. I knew that Deanna would have joined us if it hadn't been for her family responsibilities. This a problem for many female teachers. Just at the time when they are stabilized and ready to experiment at school, they are bogged down with commitments at home (Huberman, 1992).

## Giving Power to Students: Deanna

Deanna had been a member of the high school math department for at least 20 years. Her perspectives were based on an environmental history that differed from the experiences of most of the staff. As a former nun, she had taught in inner-city schools. Now the mother of three children of her own, her patient, warm, and nurturing manner with students had frequently earned her assignments that no one else wanted, such as teaching the lowest track consumer math class. She was successful with these students, however, and was always enthusiastic about what they were doing together. One of the most common phrases in her teaching repertoire was, "Come on . . . you can get the answer, you can do it." Deanna was also creative and often reflective about her successes and failures. Always receptive to new ideas, she was one of the first to use computers on a regular basis. On one occasion, after we had an animated discussion about using more cardboard cutting activities in geometry, she ran straight into her classroom to try them out.

Much of the focus of the current wave of reform is on higher standards and expectations. Unfortunately, little evidence exists that just the higher expectations of the teacher (or the government) are sufficient to effect change. Higher expectations need to be communicated to the student and supported by improved instructional strategies that increase the confirming opportunities for success. All expectations are related to goals, and goals control learning (Anderson, 1990; von Glasersfeld, 1990). But the goals or expectations of the culture must be transferred to the individual. It is not sufficient for the parent or teacher to expect the child to achieve: The child must believe he or she can.

Glasser (1986) describes a control theory axiom with a trenchant metaphor: "What students [and all of us] do in school [and out] is completely determined by the pictures in their heads" (p. 39). He believes that all children come to school with a picture that school is a satisfying place and are willing to work to achieve satisfaction. Lack of success changes the pictures in their heads—and their sense of power, which he declares is a strong human need (and goal). Teachers, parents, and peers help put and change these pictures (and goals) in children's heads.

Deanna was a good communicator. She put good pictures in her students' heads, pictures that told them she believed they could succeed. Then she provided them with the verifying experiences that *gave them new power*. Her own positive experience with previous innovations had also made her confident in her power to succeed in a new environment. A history of success with change can make educators more receptive to it (Solomon, 1977). I was therefore not surprised when Deanna supported my suggestion that tracking of students might be contributing to the department's problems.

## Choosing Support at the High School
## —and Getting It in Return

The math needs assessment group had decided that we should put most of our initial change effort into the elementary level for the benefit of long-term gains but suggested that we needed to do something about getting more students into high school math courses. This recommendation was a problem for the high school staff, although they obviously cared. At the end of the year, they anxiously graded Regents papers and expressed concern about the declining enrollment in upper-level classes.

When we addressed the results of the parent and student survey (see Chapter 3), their own responses, and the disappointing SAT and Regents exam results, the high school math teachers complained bitterly about the scope of the rigid Regents curriculum, which governed most of what they did. Jill argued cogently, "How can we teach for meaning when there is so much to cover?" They were right about the Regents curriculum. Given the limitations of a high school schedule and year, there was little time for students to construct their own knowledge. Only the most highly self-or parent-motivated students could deal with the need to rotely memorize so much abstract and unconnected material, but the exams were valued by the community and served as a difficult-to-resist standard.

This is an example of the power of the high school schedule discussed in the previous chapter, and it is another example of the double-bind messages that teachers get. Testing mandates require them to cover specific material that they frequently disfavor, which prevents them from seeking innovative approaches to the divergent situations of teaching practice. Then they are held accountable for dealing with these differing situations and needs! It is a demonstration of how the power sources of government and the public can perpetuate an unfavorable condition that is then blamed on teachers with little control.

If the public wants improvements, then curriculum and schedules need more flexibility, and teachers need more control of them. The failure to meet responsibilities is easily rationalized as someone else's fault when a person does not have control. As far as the high school staff were concerned, the source of the students' problems was external: elementary teachers' failures, insufficient time, the state-mandated curriculum and tests, students' after-school jobs, and lack of parent support in combination with the most significant cause, lack of student ability. The kids in the Regents tracks who did their homework and studied were doing fine.

This attitude of detachment from responsibility for meeting the needs of all students differs only in its degree of intensity from the disastrous hopelessness of some of my graduate students and friends who are teachers in nearby urban areas. They are frustrated because of the difficulty of dealing with a large bureaucracy as they struggle with the overwhelming needs of children from disadvantaged and disrupted homes. As long as teachers feel that they have little power to control the conditions and expectations of the teaching-learning environment, they will have good reason to refuse to accept accountability and respond to the inevitable societal changes they must face.

The high school mathematics teachers in South Vale also reflected the common conceptions of most teachers today and, unfortunately, the opinion of many of the parents. Years of using IQ tests and the culturally skewed school-related tasks they match to differentiate one student from another and then labeling these differences as inborn variations in the level of intelligence have navigated the expectations of teachers and students. In practice, teachers use its traditional measures to explain individual differences in student performance, rather than attribute these differences to the instructional process. This concept does little to provide parents or teachers with a true sense of power and distracts them from careful reflection on what they are doing. The unfortunate consequence has been the

# Evoking Change With Support and Pressure

disenfranchisement of many youngsters who, although they sometimes disprove theories and assessment of them by succeeding in real life, may never recover the advantages of a challenging education.

It seemed to the teachers to be completely out of their hands. But I was convinced that something could be done while we waited for the planned changes at the elementary levels to take effect. I knew we were stuck with the Regents standard, but couldn't we work around it? "Maybe our tracking system is partly responsible," I suggested at a department meeting. "Our labeling of students may be supporting their poor expectations and those of their parents—that may be why they are so unmotivated."

When I became more specific and suggested that we could experiment by eliminating all tracking at the ninth grade, the teachers' first reaction was predictably negative. "How can we do that—put every student in Regents level classes? Some kids just aren't born to be able to do the abstract reasoning of algebra or deal with the logic and spatial relationships of geometry. We would be dooming them to certain failure," was Gary's response. A number of his colleagues agreed with him on this.

I didn't think the idea had much of a chance to gain their support, but its timeliness in relationship to our changing school culture and some concurrent public messages about national needs and equity (including the motion picture *Stand and Deliver*) allowed my prodding to take effect. Support came from several sources. Jill, as union president, was on the DLT and had also been involved in the development of high school goals. As the teacher of the remedial lab, she was attuned to the need for higher expectations and was successful with unmotivated students. Jill was also conscientious about continuing her professional growth; she read the professional publications (often sharing them with me) and attended conferences regularly. She was highly respected by the entire staff, lived in the school district, and was the parent of two of our students. Her support for the proposal was critical in gaining its acceptance.

Alan's support was also unexpected and propitious. The high school BLT had at this point chosen higher expectations as a school-wide goal. Alan, who had become a strong opinion leader, was chairperson of the team and committed to its objectives. This collaboratively developed and shared mission was the vision that encouraged him and his department colleagues to recognize that at least a year of Regents-level mathematics (essentially algebra) was a real gatekeeper for the students.

Deanna, Alan, and Jill (and the others) did argue, rationally, that more time was needed for the less capable students. They thought it would be better to stretch the curriculum over a 2-year period. This probably was true, but I knew that at that point—because of budget constraints—we couldn't get that much more time. The high school principal would not support the year and a half alternative that some of our neighboring schools had because of scheduling difficulties. Again, the power of the schedule reigned.

I also questioned whether an extra year would differ much from our in-place concept of a year of pre-algebra. Once the sorting was effected, wouldn't we lose some of the benefits of goal equity and higher expectations? They agreed, and their power as teacher-leaders helped us reach the decision to experimentally eliminate tracking at the ninth grade. I doubt that we would have reached that decision if they had not taken ownership of the BLT goal of higher expectations.

Agreement on this decision was not unanimous, but Deanna and then, surprisingly, George were convinced enough to volunteer to work with smaller classes of students who had previously been less successful in math. Fortunately, I had some control over the allocation of resources and was able to provide each of these classes with a teaching assistant. This extra help was another form of leadership support and recognition that change requires new energies and more time. If teacher groups are to become the evocators of change, then they will need to have some control of resources and barter among themselves. They will also have to take risks. We were taking a decided risk but felt that the probability of gain outweighed the probability of loss. Being mathematicians, we gambled.

With the exception of a small group of special education students, all of the 9th and 10th graders who had not already had the Regents Level I class were assigned to it. Enrollment in Regents math classes was thereby increased to 98% at grade 9. Some of the students were in the smaller classes for support purposes, but the curriculum was the same. Every student was given the expectation that each would pass the Regents exam at the end of the year (see Steen, 1989).

The attempt to transform individual students' goals in this experiment was effective within the limitations of other variables. The program change has been maintained through time because what eventually became apparent was the long-range potential of changing the culture that communicates expectations to students and influences their individual goals. This proved to be both possible and effective. I will discuss the evidence for this further in Chapter 6.

Challenging the staff to engage in collaborative or shared decision making in both the math program change and SBCDM reform involved adapting or changing some firmly implanted cultural norms of power and control. The hope was that having more power would make teachers more secure and open to changing the way they managed instruction. Fortunately, the emerging collegial culture had begun to build the feeling of power for the math teachers. They were trusted, were empowered to make the decision and take the responsibility, and were offered the support they requested. They responded positively to my prodding as evocator and were ultimately successful! Apparent from this episode is the pattern that school cultures that allow more voice to teachers can promote productive change, especially if that culture is one in which the leader-evocator gives the necessary power and support and one in which the risks are shared.

Coincidently, as I wrote this book, the New York City teachers were about to start the new school year with the same program shift. All students were to take more challenging courses in math. Unfortunately, the decision was top-down and made late the previous spring with little preparation of the teaching staff, causing anxiety for the faculty. The teachers and the students need support to make this change successful, but it is worth a try.

## Needing Pressure

The first year of implementation of mathematics changes by volunteer piloting teachers at the elementary schools had been a successful trial. We built our capacity and generated ownership (I will describe this in Chapters 6 and 7), and we learned much from the experience. This beginning had created a microculture of peer reflection, research, and mutual support among the piloting teachers. We felt confident that this microculture would be the "critical mass" needed for systemic implementation. But the institutionalization of change rarely comes from ownership by volunteers alone, and the implementation of change becomes different when those who do not volunteer are required to participate in the process. The piloting stage of implementation of the changes in mathematics required no mandates and no pressure to become engaged. With a mandate for system-wide implementation, we were on the brink of a different sea. Because we were already moving forward at full speed, we plunged ahead! Although support for peer reflection and for capacity building was the hallmark of the first year of implementation, pressure needed to be added in the next year.

## Formative Evaluation: Making Mistakes

Piloting an educational program before implementing it in full scale has both positive and negative effects. Unless the entire school has agreed to support a pilot, it may alienate the rest of the staff, who see the pilot teachers as "favored faculty" (there was some jealousy). It may also provide the opportunity for naysayers to undermine the plan (we didn't experience this at first but did later on). Nevertheless, it is a form of action research that serves several purposes. First of all, the pilot allows the bugs to surface in a less critical and more manageable quantity. Second, if one recognizes that educational change requires personal change, it prepares people more gradually for the upheaval in their comfort level. Third, it applies a more scientific decision-making system to a process that has historically been fraught with hastily designed remedies. At least we had the beginnings of an experimental research design.

Valid evaluation research would have better controls than our pilot program did, but tight controls are close to impossible in most school situations. We made an assumption of matched groups of piloting and nonpiloting teachers at the K-3 levels. Certainly some differences existed, although probably not in the reputed strength of the individual teachers. The average age of the nonpiloters would have been older, but two of our most senior teachers were in the pilot group. Because they were volunteers, the pilot teachers were classified as greater risk takers and more receptive to new ideas. An obvious variable also intervened: Some of the nonpiloters took the in-service course we offered in the first year (Chapter 6) and began to borrow manipulatives and change their approach.

One year of program was not a long enough time to produce generalizable results (an implementation dip, which I will discuss in Chapter 8, is also possible). In real-life schools, unfortunately, there are more pressing agendas than good research. The now-published

# Evoking Change With Support and Pressure

NCTM (1989b) standards gave a clear and strong message about the need for change. Knowledgeable parents, who had heard about our change efforts, wanted their children involved, and some of the nonpiloting teachers felt left out. The students were not doing well in high school, and the media frightened educators and parents with comparisons with other countries. It would take a long time for the elementary changes to affect results at the high school. We needed to get started.

We were getting consistently good informal feedback about the trial curriculum from parents, students, teachers, and administrators but felt the need for a more objective formative program evaluation to compare it with the traditional program. The first part of this evaluation was planned by the cluster of pilot teachers for early May. It was a questionnaire addressed to all elementary and middle school staff that sought teachers' perceptions about the merits of the control (traditional) and experimental (pilot) curriculums in reference to the planning group's consensus of needs and desired outcomes. A comparison of the standardized test results attained by students in the classes with the two different curriculums would be the second measure of effectiveness.[1]

The memo accompanying the questionnaire explained the decision-making alternatives for continuation and expansion: to continue as is for another year, to expand to all K-3 classes, to add the fourth grade, or, if the evidence was clearly negative, to abandon the new program altogether. It also specified that the final decision would be an administrative one but would be based on the analysis of the questionnaire, test results, and on a feedback discussion to be held at a meeting of the entire elementary staff during a late May conference day.

It was presumptuous and typical of traditional administrators for the principals and me to think that just clarifying how the decision was to be made at this point was sufficient. Conflicts about who was in control were beginning to surface throughout the district as we engaged ever more deeply in creating a collaborative culture. The analysis of the questionnaire clearly indicated a better alignment of the new program with the planning committee's stated outcomes, but when I presented the elementary staff with these results at the conference day meeting, they engaged in a rather probing discussion about the program's merits.[2]

Although many of the nonpiloting teachers were anxious to start with the new program, a small group of others had some definite anxiety. Their concerns centered on the provision of the appropriate materials, the time that would be needed for math in an already crowded day (a reality if they were not doing much interactive teaching), the need for help in dealing with the manipulatives (they all wanted teaching assistants), and the lack of algorithmic drill and practice for students—especially in preparation for the standardized tests.

Underlying these concerns was a general resistance to change, mostly emanating from a group of three or four of the more experienced teachers (including Greta), who thought and said that this might be another innovation soon forgotten for the old-fashioned way. Huberman (1992) identifies such reactions with the career stages of "defensive focusing" or "disenchantment" (p. 129). They preferred to go on with their own special things, or they were jaded by previous and failed attempts to change them.

Their reluctance was also a function of the common discomfort with math instruction of elementary teachers, who often see themselves primarily as reading teachers. It was, in addition, a realistic concern about the publicly reported results of the standardized CAT and state competency tests—the successful performance of students on these tests using their old program had verified their successful performances as teachers. It foreshadowed the resistance to come. At the time of the meeting, the tests had been administered, but unfortunately, results were not yet available. Results actually did not arrive until after the end of the school year. Some of the anxious piloting teachers had informally checked these and felt confident that the results would support a decision to expand the program, but the strength of the test's influence was obvious. I will come back to the power of tests in Chapter 7.

Despite the concerns expressed by some of the staff at the meeting, the principals, most of the teachers, and I were convinced that the overall feedback was strong enough to make a tentative decision at the end of May to move the entire K-4 population into the new program. In early July, after we had received the test results, I consulted again with the two elementary principals. The three of us reviewed all of the feedback from the teachers and the results and finalized the decision. The timetable for this decision seemed important because materials would have to be ordered to be available for the beginning of the school year.

In retrospect, the timetable was a mistake! The elementary principals and I could not include the teachers more directly at this point

# Evoking Change With Support and Pressure 91

because they were on vacation. The decision for systemic implementation should have been left to the elementary BLTs. But old habits of role expectations die hard, and expedience seemed the priority. In the following years, some curriculum decisions were made by the BLTs. Unfortunately, as shown in Chapter 1, it is still not the norm for them to be in control of decision-making terminals.

My colleagues and I were heady with optimism from the successful trial and had learned much from the experience. We thought we had covered all bases, preparing so many intellectually for the change by involving a large group of teachers (and the principals) in the needs assessment and piloting process, by engaging everyone in the evaluation process and a 2-day preparatory workshop, and by enlisting almost half of the elementary and middle school teachers in the after-school in-service program (see Chapter 6). Before summer vacation, each teacher new to the program had also been given a teacher's guide, along with the NCTM (1989a) yearbook and a list of manipulatives from which to choose. All indications were that the district should proceed to provide every child with the opportunity to be more successful in mathematics. In actuality, we needed a little more time and a chance to hear teachers' voices in the context of their growing involvement in SBCDM.

## Understanding Resistance: Overloaded Timetables

"How can we do all of these new programs at once? And anyway, I didn't vote on this new math. The teachers who are doing it say it takes too much time and the kids don't get enough practice for the California tests. I'm going to need a teaching assistant," was Greta's reaction in the fall of the second year of implementation, when the principals and I announced that the pilot math program would be extended to all K-4 teachers. At first, only two or three teachers seemed openly resistant, all at Birch Avenue School. But their voices were loud and vehement and of concern. A single strong opinion leader such as Greta can influence the receptivity of others. A buzz of discomfort quickly spread, even to Park Lane School, which had a much larger nucleus of the pilot teachers. It is important to understand why teachers are resistant to change.

In his classic work on the sociological systems of schools, Lortie (1975) describes the characteristic needs and imperatives of teachers.

Several of these can help explain teachers' resistance. In addition to their concern for control, their "presentism," or preoccupation with the present, and their need for immediate psychic rewards, such as having reached a child or pleased a parent, deter them from more distant goals. They shy away from difficult-to-measure visions such as shared decision making and better problem-solving skills for students and veer toward the immediate feedback of a timed facts test or a worksheet. Their need to reach students also makes them bounded in their classrooms and suspicious of others' attempts to change them.

Greta's assessment of herself was dependent on these immediate rewards. Her energies were directed toward activities that provided quick and personal reinforcement, such as the feedback of corrected workbooks or the approval of parents and administrators. She was not interested in spending her time on the BLT, where she felt teachers were doing the administrator's job, or even in after-school in-service courses. Greta considered herself the expert and could foresee no rewards for the discomforts of change. And she was already on overload!

Unfortunately, concurrent curriculum demands in other areas compounded the already existing anxiety of the elementary staff. For a few teachers, the science program was new; everyone was also concerned about a new state-mandated science test. There was a new curriculum dealing with AIDS, and many teachers had to handle sex education for the first time, another new external mandate derived from the state and the community. The certified health teacher, who had done this the previous year, was eliminated from the elementary program; now they were on their own. The computer education curriculum was also revised, and their computers had been upgraded. The teaching assistant, who had carried the major burden of instruction, left and was not replaced.

I addressed the elementary teachers at a meeting on opening day of the 1989-1990 school year with a list of these changes and heard an undercurrent of anxious groans. An apropos colloquialism describing their reaction is "Give us a break." The promise of workshops early in the year did not help much. Each of these areas and the new mathematics program were particularly uncomfortable for most elementary teachers who saw themselves as more expert in the language arts.

Most of the teachers in this group were experienced and mature people, certainly capable of handling these changes. The imposition of these new things, however, was a real threat to their comfort and success with past practices. It wasn't that they hadn't had an opportunity to become involved in the process. They could have participated in the math or computer needs assessment clusters that recommended the changes, been involved in the AIDS committee that met with community participants, or worked on the science changes (a few teachers did). Becoming involved in these clusters were additions to their existing workloads—and their energies were directed toward their own classrooms. Given the opportunity, they would not have made a choice to do all of this at once. But neither were they ready to sacrifice the time and energy needed to reflect with others, so that they could have made wise choices and set reasonable timetables for themselves.

Teachers should not have to make such sacrifices! Their problems with the discomforts of change are compounded by the perceived loss of control. They feel powerless and overburdened with new things they never wanted—often all at the same time! Resistance to change will continue until the time and energy required for shared decision making becomes a valued and rewarded component of the teaching profession, and teachers have more control over timetables. Those timetables, however, must meet the needs of the children and the community they serve. In a productively functioning social system, responsibility connects with control.

## A Balance of Support and Pressure

Just as a student brings a whole individual set of previous informal experiences to a learning situation, so do leaders and those they lead bring disparate histories to the change process. The situation-bound contexts of time and leadership power, as manifested in the control of others and in the distribution of resources to and by that leader, are of decided impact on efforts to transform schools. Even when leadership is consistent, the interacting individuals will have different histories and be subject to different situational forces. Greta, Alan, and Elaine (who were described in the previous chapter) were not at all alike. A variety of motivations therefore must be considered in efforts to implement change. The motivations depend on the needs of the individual, on the particular school history and climate, and on the nature of the interaction between the leader or peer evocator of change and the teacher.

The first few months of systemwide implementation of the changes in mathematics at South Vale required intensive support from administrators and the peers who had been in the original pilot. When it became necessary to convince those who were reluctant to change that the change was now mandated, that pages of drill and practice would be assigned for organized abandonment (Spady & Marshall, 1990), and that monitoring would occur, pressure was also called into action. Power enables pressure, but pressure applied to human beings without a cushion of support is doubtful in its return of value. A carefully balanced and individualized combination of pressure and support was critical in this implementation phase (Cox, 1983; Crandall, 1983; Miles, 1983). Administrators and peers had already provided some support. Pressure was now needed.

## Meg

The need for pressure began with an inevitable confrontation between Greta and Meg, her principal at the Birch Avenue School. Meg had come to South Vale in its first year of SBCDM, but it was not her first principalship. She was an experienced, secure, and caring principal, much admired by her staff, administrative colleagues, and parents. The Birch Avenue staff was more resistant, more mature, untrusting, and less interested in increasing their control (especially if it meant more work) than the Park Lane staff. Most of the Birch Avenue teachers were, like Greta, at the stages of their careers when they were defensively focusing on their own comfortable specialties or disenchanted with previous top-down efforts to infringe on them.

As a nontenured newcomer, Meg faced a real challenge with this staff. Her experience paid off. Her leadership style leaned heavily toward consideration, or the giving of power and support. She spent much of her time in classrooms, and on Monday mornings she gathered all of the children in the auditorium so that the teachers could share breakfast together. She even baked for them! Sparked by her own background as a science teacher, she accompanied me to a 3-day conference to investigate a new science program. We brought it back to the teachers, and, with her support and theirs, we implemented it with ease.

## Evoking Change With Support and Pressure

But when pressure was needed, Meg was right there. When Greta and a few others tried to bypass the new program by making copies of drill and practice activities from old texts that abrogated the new goals in mathematics, she monitored the copy machine and restricted its use for this purpose. Her use of power in this manner precipitated a major reaction that reverberated throughout the district. This type of censorship control had never been applied before, and teachers reacted strongly to the infringement on their classroom power. There were several frantic calls from the piloting teachers, principals, and Jim, the assistant superintendent, who was not that supportive. After all, he had not been there for the entire process and was busy with his own visions.

We needed to deal with the entire situation. Jim and the teachers needed to be informed. All of us had to support each other. The principals and I prepared a memo that included a chronology of what had transpired in the change process during the previous 2 years. It clearly outlined the district's expectations and reminded everyone of how teachers had had an opportunity to become involved at each step. Although the timetable was too fast and the final determination to proceed was a traditional administrative decision terminal, we had listened carefully to their voices, and we wanted to remind them of that. The teachers also received a copy of a page from the NCTM (1989b) standards to demonstrate that what was proposed was what their professional colleagues had decided was appropriate and necessary.

This memo served several purposes in addition to applying some pressure at a crucial moment. It succinctly stated our own and the professional culture's current philosophy, as well as indicators of its fulfillment. Too often schools are vague about philosophy. If it exists in writing, it is disconnected from the specific suggested practices that would represent its manifestation.

The memo worked! Although there was still much to be done to provide the necessary support to overcome the more passive resistance to change—remember, we were no longer working with volunteers—the overt and vocal resistance briefly heard in teachers' lunchrooms and even at a faculty meeting disappeared. It erupted only once again, when we first presented our timetable for the criterion-referenced tests. Just as Sarason (1972) has cautioned, the timetables that leaders set create anxiety and pressure. In this case, pressure and support were the leader's remedy.

## Using Pressure in a Supportive Way

Together, Meg and I applied pressure in more supportive ways, trying to overcome resistance by demonstrating the children's needs or alerting teachers to their needs for greater capacity. When Edith had problems accepting and implementing the new approach, Meg asked me to help. Edith, an experienced and hard-working teacher, complained that she was having difficulty with the whole program and that it "wasn't working for her." Rather than observing her and making suggestions, I modeled a lesson and followed up with an analysis of what I did and why I did it. This led finally, although subtly, to suggestions on how she might change her teaching strategies. The modeling was valuable because Edith was not threatened by an observation of what she was doing. Seeing her own students learn in the manner we suggested proved that it could be done. I will discuss the use of model lessons in building teachers' capacity further in the following chapters.

In contrast to Park Lane School, in which the piloting teachers became the strong evocators for change, the success of the math program at Birch Avenue School is doubtless a result of Meg's persistence. The school staff has recently been almost completely turned over. Time will tell whether or not their level of collegial leadership can reach that of Park Lane.

The need for pressure by leaders that was required in the systemic adoption phase of the mathematics program change was traditional. Our expectations would have to be made clear: Once there was collegiality in the decision-making process and generous support, no one would duck from the responsibility to make a legitimate attempt to accomplish the agreed-on program goals. Ultimately, in later phases when the culture had changed, any needed external pressure would come from the influence of formally and informally shared peer reflections. The internal pressure to succeed with their students that energizes the actions of most teachers would take over (see below and Chapter 7).

As Hopkins (1990) discovered, "Change in teacher behavior is the result of a dialectic between specific and general motivation, between individual motivation and school climate" (p. 62). Some teachers are self-motivated to make adjustments in response to reflections about a specific problem or have a general openness to the search for improvement. Some respond to competition with peers or the wish to be part of the team; others respond only to formal authority.

It is a mistake to rely totally on formal authority. The difficulties faced by the California schools, in which changes in mathematics education have been mandated but not necessarily implemented, demonstrate that policy changes are not sufficient to assure follow-through by teachers (Darling-Hammond, 1990). In South Vale, we faced some resistance to policy change because we had made some mistakes with time and process, but we diminished the difficulties by giving and using some of our preserves of power. Teachers and administrators influenced others by paying attention to their voices, engaging them in decision making, providing them with support in many forms, and applying pressure when needed. In the chapters ahead, I will describe the support that is needed for gaining new capacity and suggest how ownership and the continuity of cultural change are assured with documented curriculum and assessments.

## The Pressure of New Roles

The transition to site-based management was similarly "situational," but the requirements of new roles and shifts in power made the transformations much more difficult. The changes would influence the informal culture, which French and Bell (1973) have described as including "feelings, informal actions and interactions, group norms, and values" (p. 17). Who does what to whom became an important issue. Effecting changes in the informal culture may be subject to more intense versions of the same constraining variables as changing the conceptual realities of the students. Tightly held concepts have to be reconstructed, and the task of bringing each individual and each group to a new consensus is complex.

For example, teachers and principals have well-established, though usually unstated, role definitions for themselves. These role definitions involve informal and commonly understood norms for the distribution of power. Teachers accept supervision and evaluation by principals, but their group norm is not to assess the performance of their peers; consequently, they are hesitant to accept group accountability. Principals are reluctant to relinquish decision-making terminals to teachers. Principals do not believe teachers understand the pressures principals endure from other power preserves that they, and not the teachers, are accountable to, such as central office, parents, boards of education, and state departments of education.

There was no real pressure of a bottom line for teachers in the change to site-based management. Any teacher could sit on the sidelines while others grappled for them. The principals, however, were expected to engage in the process—a process designed to deprive them of traditional power. Two principals from other districts have recently told me that they are thinking of retiring because they cannot deal with the loss of control that is attached to the New York State mandate for shared decision making. I suggested that they wait for a while to see what happens. The problem for everyone in the South Vale case was the lack of consistent leadership vision and support. We were ahead of our time; perhaps it will be there for them.

## When Leadership Support Is Missing

Although it started out with great promise, the course toward greater voice for teachers in decision making was not easy in South Vale. In addition to an inconsistent vision and the conflict over power and control, leadership support from central office was missing. Little mitigated the drain on the limited preserve of everyone's energies for this new purpose. At first, teachers on the building teams were enthusiastically occupied with the improvement plans that responded to the annual needs assessments and analyses of their test results. They designed and implemented a broad range of activities that at first focused on the physical environment but soon included changes in reward systems and parent communications, interdisciplinary experiences, a clarification of objectives, and mentoring programs for students. They made exhaustive direct reports about these efforts to the board of education and their own colleagues.

In the second and third years, however, the BLT teacher-leaders began to complain overtly about the stress of the paper work and reporting responsibilities. Some teachers replaced the original members on the teams, but still a sizable number of the faculty were disinterested and uninvolved. The satisfaction of accomplishment of those who labored was tempered by an underlying perception that they had gained little real control. Some of this was because at the same time that they were making some minor gains in building level control, new mandates were making incursions into areas previously under their power: their day-to-day instructional decisions. Their frustration was intensified by the confusion about the range and

# Evoking Change With Support and Pressure

limits of the decisions they could make, and no one was there to lead them toward consensus (Barth, 1988).

Clarity, congruence, and consistency were missing from this vision of cultural change. Did every teacher have to vote on the new math program, or was the decision of the representative cluster based on everyone's feedback sufficient? Did administrators have the right to extend the decision of a representative group to others? Who would decide when extended team meetings took place or what the agenda would be? Was just making recommendations for major conference days enough—especially if they weren't always followed? What if a fourth-grade teacher did not want to teach an introduction to sex education as part of the new mandate for AIDS education from the state education department?

State-mandated curricula and tests that monitor their outcomes are constant sources of external and internal pressure for educators. They create external pressure because they are imposed without direct teacher involvement yet generate a sense of obligatory compliance. Teachers are sensitive to the anxieties of parents with whom they privately share results, and they respond to the concerns of the community with whom group results are publicly shared. Tests create internal pressure because they are a source of personal affirmation for conscientious teachers—they need to measure their own personal success. Only the support of leaders who help teachers build their capacity and power can help balance this pressure.

## Holding on to Power and Reneging on Promises

As I described above, at South Vale the high school schedule interfered with implementation of what the math teachers thought best for the students. Many of the ideas of the high school BLT in other areas were also constrained by the schedule. Everyone's reluctance to abandon previously rewarding practices was a real problem, but the lack of consistent leadership support, particularly that of the giving of power, was the major one.

By the third year of SBCDM implementation, the board of education in South Vale was different from the one in charge at the beginning. The superintendent, unfortunately, had little power with this new board. He was scheduled to leave within the year. Jim, the assistant superintendent, was in his second year, had his own visions, and hoped that the board would choose him as the replacement. The new board of education was in charge!

As I have mentioned, the visions of the board and the teachers were never congruent. The board was delighted and impressed by the many wonderful activities reported by the BLTs but saw the SBCDM reform only as a way to get more effective schools—not as a way to give more power to teachers. Using their power in an economy move, the board decided to encumber space at the high school for central office administrative purposes and rent out the separate facility. Board members also felt that increasing the proximity of the central office to the high school would enhance supervision. The superintendent was against this idea but was only able to convince them to engage the high school BLT in a fact-finding exploration of the impact on the high school facilities.

The response of the board of education was disappointing. After the high school BLT collected data and made a cohesive and convincing presentation that represented a unanimous recommendation not to move the facility, the board decided to do it anyway. This was seen by the teachers as an indication of their true powerlessness. "How could they do that! Ask us to do the work and come up with a recommendation, and then ignore it!" The underlying purpose of increasing supervision was also perceived by teachers as a lack of trust. This decision was the most serious setback for the collaborative process in its first 3 years of implementation.

Indeed, public education, subject as it is to the politics of annual elections of board members and voter budget approval, is more constrained by community pressures than most teachers even realize. They see their administrators as the power brokers. Involving the teachers in making the schools more effective did not mean that the boards were ready to relinquish their responsibility to keep taxes down, and they certainly were not ready to hand over control of the schools to teachers.

## Commitment and the Support of Tangible Resources

Limited access to resources constrained teachers' power: District funds for leadership team planning time, supplies, support from teaching assistants, and class sizes were not in the teachers' control. Money brings power! Providing tangible resources is a way to provide support. The district's financial investment in the SBCDM process was essentially minimal. Some special funding from the state paid for many of the activities and freed the district from the need to spend money for this purpose. It was a good deal but may also have diminished its commitment. Soft money from grant programs often fails to build local loyalties.

Budgeting from these funds for the building teams' efforts was limited to the costs of outside consultants, substitute teachers for the district planning team, overtime pay for the summer work of the building teams, and refreshments. The money was controlled and allocated by central administration. Building teams had no opportunity to build their own budgets and use money as they saw fit to make significant changes in their instructional delivery systems. Administrators did some bartering, granting little bits of power in exchange for involvement. But most of the principals were not yet ready to back off, nor were teachers ready to take responsibility for others.

A process that had been in place for many years proved both productive and frustrating. Each year, as part of the budget development process, individuals were encouraged to submit proposals for new or changed programs directly to the board of education. The building teams used this system to make suggestions for changes that had budgetary implications. Several of the elementary BLTs made eloquent and well-prepared presentations at budget hearings.

Some of the teams' recommendations to provide funds for program improvements were granted, but the larger turned-down number proved disillusioning. When the high school BLT was successful with some of its recommendations, the elementary teams saw favoritism. It was difficult for the teachers to accept the cost limits and begin to look at trade-offs in a productive way. Nor were the board of education and district management, for that matter, ready to defer their own priorities for those of the leadership teams.

In Reitzug's (1994) terms, this was providing autonomy without possibility, a teasing and frustrating combination! A better structure that would provide site-based control of some resources within a predetermined limit was needed. Teachers need to understand budgetary limits better and compete creatively within themselves for what is available, but they also need the motivation of control to do this.

## How Leadership Power and Evocator Support Make the Difference

In this chapter and the preceding one, I discussed the different sources of leadership power and some of the ways in which power is managed (given or used) to support, pressure for, or prevent the changes we envision. I have not yet addressed the role of support in increasing teachers' capacity or demonstrated how this increased capacity can add to the individual teacher's power and overcome resistance. Certain patterns have emerged, however, and need to be crystallized:

- Leadership for change can emerge from many sources: administrators, teacher groups, and individual teachers.
- Leaders need power, which they may either use for control or give to others.
- Traditional holders of power are reluctant to relinquish it.
- Responsibility for oneself and others must accompany control.
- Change requires upheavals in the patterns of giving and using power. Consistency of leadership or consensus of vision is therefore significant.
- Support implies the giving of power in such forms as voice, autonomy, trust, and energy expended by the leader-evocator.
- Pressure implies the using of power, but it should be accompanied by some giving and support energy expended by the leader.
- Both pressure and support need to be accompanied by leadership actions such as providing opportunities for peer reflections, wandering around, asking questions, providing a broad range of staff development activities including modeling, and providing tangible (such as money) and intangible (such as time) rewards (further detail ahead).
- Double-bind messages, reneging on promises, and teacher overloads increase resistance. Teachers in control of their own timetables may be less resistant.
- Within the above patterns, each situation is different and may require different balances of support and pressure.

The situations were different for South Vale's two concurrent changes. The mathematics effort had consistency of leadership and

# Evoking Change With Support and Pressure

a combination of pressure and support that leaned heavily on the support and giving of power. There was change but little negative impact on the cultural norms of roles. Money for change was more or less under my control as curriculum director, the evocator of change—it was mostly hard (local budget) money (although Eisenhower funds paid for some of the formal staff development). The change infringed on teacher imperatives. Resistance came from some of those who were mandated to change, but it was overcome with much support and some pressure.

In the change toward greater voice for teachers in decision making (SBCDM), leadership was inconsistent, although it arose from unexpected sources. There was little giving of power and little support. Money was mostly soft (a state grant) and not in the control of site-based teams. Pressure to participate was only on the principals. The cultural norms of roles were affected. Resistance came from traditional holders of power, who also held the imperative of responsibility.

A critical effect that offers great promise for the new wave of reform is important to note. Although it was not always positive, there was interaction between the changes. The curriculum change in mathematics was supported by the change in school governance. In the chapter ahead, readers will also see how, with and without the support of leaders, teachers increased their capacity in both of these reforms, and with it their power and their ability to lead and influence their students and others.

## Notes

1. The CAT did not measure the conceptual breadth of our new curriculum, but we used it as a minimum standard for evaluation of concepts, which were separately recorded from computation. Surprisingly, when compared with the previous year's results, there was little loss of computation skill and an expected gain in concepts, but neither was significant. I will describe the development of our own tests in Chapter 7.

2. There was a significant difference between the experimental and control teacher group responses ($t = 3.73$, $p = .005$). The new program was judged more useful as a guide for concrete developmental activities, concrete to pictorial to symbolic transitions, motivating students, challenging students to explain and understand what they are doing, and applying that understanding to problem solving. It was also judged as closer to our goals in its time spent in interactive versus seat work activities.

# 6

# Changing People
## *The Power of New Capacity*

### About Changing People

Schools are organizations with formal structures. These structures have been compared to the top parts of an iceberg. Underneath the surface, schools are grounded by the much less visible structures of the informal culture (French & Bell, 1973). People with different needs, feelings, and experiences form this culture; if these are not attended to, the chances for true organizational change are diminished. Visions of educational change need to be transferred to teachers, administrators, and parents: It is the people of schools who must change, and they may be resistant.

For example, humans have strong needs to control the environment and preserve what has in the past brought satisfaction and comfort. It is difficult to displace practices that satisfy teachers' needs to feel successful. They have to be convinced that although what they have been doing was appropriate for a different time and place, it no longer fits and that greater satisfaction for themselves as teachers can indeed be achieved with a new practice. They need to take ownership of this new practice and abandon some of what previously made them comfortable.

If changing schools hinges on changing people, then improving what schools do implies the building of new capacity for those who carry out its purpose. Somehow, leaders have to help teachers such as Greta gain the power of new capacity and achieve the new rewards that will enable them to abandon their comfortable, but ineffective, practices. Principals such as Anne have to learn how to listen to the voices around them and how to share their power. Parents have to understand the value of methods that are different from those they experienced and expect.

Building new capacity for educators (and their students) is a major task, a variable of change in the action path of reflective practice that requires the energies of those who must increase their capacity and those who lead them. Building capacity requires the leader-evocator's energy in each category of support that was described in the preceding chapter. It is, however, a rewarding task because new capacity is enabling, bringing new power to those who have grown. As South Vale proceeded with the manifestation of its visions of transformation, we discovered capacity to be a variable of great strength, attenuated only by the time it took to accrue. Capacity can promote ownership, counteract the inhibiting forces of history and inconsistency of leadership, mitigate the struggle for power and control, and diminish the need for pressure. Capacity can overcome resistance!

The final three chapters in this examination of school change will focus on the building of new capacity. This chapter explores the tradition of staff development and the consequences of inadequate maps for building new capacity and then suggests a template of mechanisms for helping educators reach a first stage of competency. Chapter 7 considers the role of curriculum and assessment in helping them reach the second stage of expertise, comfort and power, and then briefly addresses the concomitant need for new capacity for parents. Chapter 8 proposes that time may either increase capacity or cause it to wither away. These three chapters also take readers from the implementation stage to the maintenance stage of the process of change.

## New Capacity for Teachers: Professional Development

Teachers and parents have not been trained to manage schools, and administrators have not been trained to share their leadership. Little is really known about how to work as collegial teams; a research base that would inform educators is just evolving. The knowledge of the process of learning is older and more extensive, but basic research on how learning takes place has not usually been the guide for instruction. Although, intuitively, individual teachers and their leaders were often right, choices of preferred instructional strategies by educators were sometimes based on other factors such as fashion, habit, comfort, tradition, and cost.

The process through which educational leaders have attempted to construct new skills for practicing educators or rebuild their existing instructional strategies has traditionally been called staff development. The concept of development, when applied in the Piagetian sense to young children, implies a naturally occurring, self-generated process. This is, however, far from what have been the standard methods prescribed for increasing teachers' capacity. Formal, top-down-initiated in-service programs, workshops, and supervisory feedback attached to evaluation procedures have been the in-house practice norm for developing teachers' skills—or schools depended on reward systems for the teacher's participation in separate, sometimes unrelated, university-based graduate programs.

Recently, the scope of what is now viewed as professional development has been enlarged. Joyce and Showers' (1980) description, for example, identified five components of the process: "presentation, modeling, practice, feedback and coaching" (p. 380). As defined by Little (1992), professional development goes beyond these and includes any activity that is intended to improve teachers' skills, attitudes, or performance. Listening to them is a good place to begin.

Concurrent with increasing attention to the involvement of teachers in governance, there is also concern for more voice and control of the professional development process by teachers. Hopkins (1990) relates the success of staff development programs to the climate of the school and the personality of the teacher. His findings correlate successful embedding of new practices with a high degree of teacher self-actualization and open school cultures with greater receptivity for change initiation. Goodson (1992) asserts "that particularly in the world of teacher development what is missing is the teacher's voice.... What is needed is a focus that listens above all to the person at whom development is aimed" (p. 114).

Glatthorn (1987) offers peer cooperation or dialogue in small groups as a staff development approach. Fullan (1990) links peer reflection among teachers, with collective action and open cultures, to successful implementation of change in schools. The importance of social interactions and peer influence in the learning process has been the subject of research and extensive application in the instructional approach of cooperative learning, which followed the landmark work of Johnson, Johnson, and Johnson-Holubec (1987) and Johnson and Johnson (1989). In South Vale, an increase in peer interactions among students was a vital component of the vision for mathematics education; peer reflections among teachers was the hallmark of the transformation that helped us to reach that vision.

Stenhouse (1985) sees the "teacher as researcher" and concludes that "ideas and people are not of much use until they are digested to the point where they are subject to the teacher's own judgment" (p. 104). Louden (1992) also attaches shared research to teacher development and the reflective process. In an attempt to understand reflection as a participant in the action of teaching, he demonstrates an example of a teacher reflecting collaboratively with a researcher. In South Vale, sharing personal observations and experiences, as well as comparisons with those of others, provided direction for the district's endeavors to change the way mathematics was taught. Shared research engaged, increased, and refined our capacities. Analyses of our own research-based assessments were, in fact, the turning point in the institutionalization of the change (see Chapter 7). Joyce, Bennett, and Bennett (1990) caution, however, that "reorienting school cultures toward collegial problem solving, and study and incorporation of advances in research in curriculum and teaching has turned out to be difficult" (p. 33).

The nature of professional development must respond to the knowledge of how learning takes place and of how teachers' actions are determined. New knowledge is not constructed until each individual has reformed or adapted prior knowledge; the processing of new perceptions from research, verbal interactions with peers, and reflections in the process of doing are the settings for these adaptations. Constructivists such as Piaget (1977) and von Glasersfeld (1990) attribute the advantage of human interactions in the learning process to the greater likelihood of disequilibrium followed by new self-constructed knowledge and to the power of goals as controllers. Cognitive scientists who study information processing, such as Anderson (1990), add greater opportunity for new sensory input and new perceptions causing new brain adaptations to the explanation.

My experience as an evocator of change makes me most comfortable with the broader, inclusive, and bottom-up descriptions of how

## Changing People: The Power of New Capacity

professional development should occur. Although I have used all of the Joyce and Showers components at times, it is through the reflective process—sometimes the teacher reflecting alone, sometimes with peers, sometimes with evocator mediation, and sometimes on structured research—that I have seen transformation occur most easily.

The evocator's role as prodder, map maker, and mediator of the process of change can be compared with that of the expert in an apprenticeship relationship. The evocator may be a leader mediating many interactions but may also be a peer expert acting as a coach to one individual. I remember my frustration with dropped stitches when I was learning to knit and my increased understanding of the procedure as a consequence, but having my sister around to help me deal with the problem gave me the direction and encouragement I needed.

No matter how well the expert plans with and for the apprentice, however, the best learning is in the doing. Teachers talking, planning, researching, and evaluating with each other and with experts are reflecting *on* action. Then, as they practice, they are reflecting *in* action (Schön, 1983). Both stages of reflection are at the functional level of change. Shared reflections may be among peers of equal expertise with a new practice or between a peer who has had some extra training or experience and one who has not.

For the past 4 years, as part of a funded graduate program at St. Thomas Aquinas College in New York, a succession of teachers from many school districts have become involved in intensive summer institutes that prepare them to be experts at constructivist math and science and to be mentors or peer coaches for others who receive only minimal preparation. In most of these cases, what has started out as an apprentice-expert relationship has matured to become one in which there is equality of input, with mutual give and take of feedback, ideas, and materials.[1] The growth in capacity that leads to equality of interaction results from practice with reflection in action followed by peer reflection on action.

The notable difference of this program when compared with traditional university-based programs is that the capacity-building interactions between peers are structured. The added value for any apprentice-expert relationships in the practice of an art or skill is that the learning process for gaining new capacity is not haphazard. It is usually carefully mapped.

## Developing the Capacity to Manage Collaboratively

The challenge for South Vale educators involved in site-based leadership teams and their concurrent involvement in implementing new strategies for teaching mathematics required maps for the acquisition of new knowledge and new skills. Unfortunately, the teachers and principals on the leadership teams had little formal mapping by experts for their new shared management roles, either before or during the implementation of change. One reason for this, of course, was that this was breaking new ground. No experts and little research base existed.

Another reason for the missing map, which has been discussed in previous chapters, was a lack of power, support, and consistent leadership. After negotiating with Jim, the assistant superintendent, the BLTs were offered some short-term seminars in group dynamics, but the seminars were far from adequate. The teams had to depend on systematized engagement in peer reflection. Beginning with the summer planning sessions and continuing with meetings throughout the school year, the teams slowly gained capacity and momentum while facing the reality that despite expectations for improvements on the basis of the yearly needs assessments, little support would come from the central office and not enough would develop from their colleagues.

The teams were expected to pay more attention to outcomes and become proactive in the education of their peers. Outcomes were based on socioeconomically disaggregated analyses (see Chapter 3) of the standardized tests. They neither understood nor valued these analyses. The connections between student outcomes and the improvements they planned in response to the closed-ended needs assessments, such as cleaning up the physical environment and planning and engaging in schoolwide activities, were not always clear or as direct as they would have preferred. Even the BLTs' involvement with hiring new staff seemed indirect and frustrating when their choices were overruled by principals or central office.

Engaging students in interdisciplinary schoolwide activities, for example, seemed to some teachers to have little impact on the tests and interfered with the time they saw as necessary for their own agendas. Direct effects on students were clearer when they began to improve student reward systems and discipline procedures and changed the way they communicated with parents.

# Changing People: The Power of New Capacity

In general, however, the school leadership teams struggled to gain the capacity to build the trust of their colleagues, administrators, the board of education, and parents; to encourage teachers to risk their time and energy; to convince the district management to risk its resources; and to persuade principals to risk their power. Amidst all of this struggle, however, was evidence that backward steps from the inchoate restructured culture would be difficult. Those teachers who had been involved in building leadership teams and contributed in a positive way gained a sense of professionalism and a degree of self-actualization, which for a long time would condition them to strive for greater roles in the decision-making process.

At first, this struggle may have been only for the rewards of the community of discourse: a chance to reflect and share joy and pain with colleagues, or perhaps even for the opportunity to complain to the principal under the protective blanket of common cause. Nevertheless, with time, practice, and small but important gains in their own capacity to plan and come to consensus, the BLTs began to shape a professional culture. Although it was still generally a received culture with limited empowerment because the forum and resources were externally controlled (Cooper, 1988), it was a culture with a developing corps of teacher-leaders.

## Belonging to the Team: Ownership

During the first 4 years, there was enough respect for membership on the BLT in some schools to attract more than the planned number of members. In other schools, teachers who were not ready to risk their effort for what they saw as long-range, intangible, or unnecessary payoffs abdicated their responsibility to participate but accepted the decisions of their peers—sometimes without questions and sometimes with grumbles about the "extra" or "make work" demands.

A new energy in the day-to-day discourse among teachers, however, resolved educational problems and suggested solutions more often than had previously occurred. The lunchroom conversations frequently turned to successful instructional strategies. Some after-school conferences became workshops rather than merely information-receiving sessions. This was coupled (after 2 years of concentration on the school environments) with a growing pride in the buildings, in the students, and in each other's accomplishments. Elaine (at Park Lane School) expressed the opinion of many in these words: "I felt so proud to be a member of this staff."

Most significant, the sense of isolation diminished. Team members had begun to recognize the importance of collegiality in overcoming what Lieberman, Saxl, and Miles (1988) call the "powerful infantilizing effects" (p. 151) of many school cultures. Alan, the high school teacher I described in Chapter 4, is a good example of a new maturity for those involved. But even those who were already secure and successful benefited. Hannah, a beloved high school English teacher, adviser to the literary magazine, BLT member, and one of the most student-centered (as opposed to subject-centered) high school teachers I know, surprised us with her comment: "I love discussing school problems with my colleagues. It makes me feel like an adult, and important."

## Sandy

Sandy was a highly respected middle school teacher and an avid member of the BLT from the start. A consummate professional, organized, caring, and giving, Sandy was an exceptional teacher who never ceased to grow and share her new knowledge. Her birthday was a cause for everyone's celebration, and placement in her classes was the gift of a lifetime for students. As a member of an instructional team of outstanding sixth-grade teachers, she helped set the standard that lifted us all. Sandy overcame her unassuming personality to become the district's evocator of cooperative learning and creative writing. She also carried the major responsibility for the middle school BLT and was of great assistance to Richard, the new principal.

One outstanding activity is a good example of the power of her inspiration and leadership and the potential of teacher-leaders in a collegial culture. The BLT, which had chosen interdisciplinizing curriculum as a priority that year, organized a schoolwide focus on the Olympics. Curriculum adjustments and activities in every subject area addressed this theme. The project culminated in a day of schoolwide events managed mostly by Marge, another strong team member. The events took a great deal of cooperative planning, but most staff members caught the spirit and contributed.

## The Cause of Burnout

This team had several major accomplishments. They followed up the Olympics' interdisciplinary curriculum project with a Renaissance theme, planned and implemented a mentor program for needy kids, organized two programs for parents, and continued extensive efforts to provide awards and incentives for teachers and students. Their goal to share objectives and goals with students had good staff compliance. In some respects, they were ahead of the other teams.

It soon became apparent, however, that such energy would not have been generated without the few of them doing so much. Sandy privately complained to me that a few isolated individuals did nothing and that the principal did not help with these staff members. As she became more involved in sharing her knowledge and skill in cooperative learning, she struggled vainly to get others to take her place. Soon Sandy justifiably complained that there was neither compensation nor relief from her effort. She had to type the school building improvement plans herself and pleaded, "Even one period a week less of lunch duty would help." She had difficulty engaging staff on the team because they "don't think it's worth the effort, and some say you are just working for administration for free."

The original team was just burned out, and no takers replaced them. Perhaps it was the missing rewards for participation or the complacency of many staff members with the status quo. Perhaps it was lack of trust. They used the team to deal with a communication gap with the assistant principal but were reluctant to risk dealing with another school problem. The team's growth in capacity to manage was not sufficient to bring them the power they needed to sustain and recruit the required investment of energy, and additional power did not come to them from other sources. The passing of time would offer the new energies of newly hired teachers, but as readers shall see in Chapter 8, they brought little capacity and power with them.

## Becoming Problem Solvers

SBCDM did begin to move South Vale from a "problem hiding" to a "problem solving" organization (McLaughlin & Yee, 1988, p. 30).

Sandy complained, however, "We don't do enough problem solving; Richard doesn't want our meetings to be gripe sessions." Another principal expressed this frustration: "They just complain, they don't want to do anything productive." This was a reflection of the lack of congruence in visions and everyone's lack of capacity. Teachers did not connect their new roles to the burden of new accountability; principals did. It takes little energy and capacity to complain about what is wrong but much of both to design and implement ways to make things right. Principals needed to know how to share their power and transform negative feelings into positive actions. Central office administrators needed the capacity to provide them with the necessary support.

Building and district leadership teams were involved in the hiring of new teaching staff and administrators (including a new superintendent), but the decision terminals of final choices were not in their power; they were disillusioned when some individuals they had not favored were hired, whereas those they recommended were not. They had a role in determining class composition; in deciding a few minor schedule revisions; in changing the student discipline, monitoring, and reporting systems; and, as I described in Chapter 5, in actively planning and presenting new program additions as part of the budgetary process. The two secondary teams planned special personal counseling programs for students in need of extra adult time and convinced many of their less-involved colleagues to volunteer their time to work in the programs.

Much of the leadership teams' initial efforts concentrated on the effective schools criteria of safe and orderly environment, rewards and incentives, monitoring student progress, and high expectations. The use of these criteria may have served to delay a focus on the other "stuff of teaching and learning" (Little, 1988, p. 84), the choices about curriculum and instruction. This delay may have also been the result of the existence of the several concurrent, vertical, and districtwide collegial clusters, including the needs assessment teams and separate staff development and effective strategies committees. All of these dealt with curriculum (see Chapter 2). The needs assessments were part of the responsibility of the curriculum directors whose roles were not specifically functional in the early site-based plans. They, in turn, proceeded to engage staff in the curriculum process without regard to individual building plans, which concentrated on other diagnosed needs.

# Changing People: The Power of New Capacity

In the fourth year, the annual building-level needs assessment became much more open-ended in an attempt to widen the focus; curriculum then became a major consideration, at least in the elementary and middle schools. As the energies of the building teams shifted more toward the instructional program, some consolidation of the vertical clusters was eventually effected. The BLTs began to take over some of the curriculum process and included the directors as consultants. The Park Lane team made a special effort to document goals and objectives in every area. The revision of social studies curriculum, for example, was a site-based activity they accomplished with the guidance of the curriculum director. Elementary building plans ultimately began to consider the district curriculum cycle and incorporate it into the activities. As I will describe ahead, continuity in the math program change is more likely because of this integration. There may be an advantage, however, in having a variety of ad hoc collegial clusters. Indeed, I regret that the role of the curriculum director has been diluted by budgetary constraints and the site-based process. I will discuss the ramifications of this later in the book.

## Becoming Accountable for Each Other

In South Vale, we did not approach the medical model of a professional culture because the teams never considered such things as peer review or engendered enough trust from their colleagues to risk proposing regular and teacher-structured programs of peer observation and modeling, a "bellwether practice" (Little, 1988, p. 87) that would signal the further diminution of isolation and provide a more responsive process then existing administrative feedback. Some small steps were taken in that direction, however. In the second year, individual teachers participated in and appreciated the peer observation and coaching component of the TESA training (Kerman, 1979), which I mentioned in Chapter 2. In the third year, a few teachers finally volunteered for demonstrations of math lessons. In the fifth and sixth years, several of the experienced staff became mentors for a group of new teachers. The openness of the experienced group to accepting this role corresponded to their increased capacity to interact in a professional way with peers, their knowledge of the value of this interaction, and their acceptance of accountability for others (I will describe their activities in reference to the mathematics changes later).

Despite the ease with which most teachers engage in peer reflections and informal teacher-to-teacher coaching when they are offered the possibility, teachers find it difficult to become trusting enough to be comfortable with the concept of a formal role that implies a peer evaluative activity, even when the expert is the experienced teacher and the novice is a beginner. As I mentioned previously, the tendency is for peers to quickly slip into the equal input mode when engaged in peer reflective activities.

Teachers are also reluctant to give the time and energy for this purpose. Some teams' building improvement plans delegated responsibility to the principal for providing opportunities for peer observation by interested parties. The purpose of this may have been a beginning recognition of the value of such interaction. It may also have been an indication of the staff's unwillingness to use their "own" time for such activities, suggesting instead that they be relieved by the principal of classroom duties for this professional endeavor. This shifting of responsibility away from the teachers sets up a conflict for the principal, who must balance the long-term benefits of peer observation with the immediate loss of teacher-student interaction time. In a true professional culture, teacher-to-teacher reflective interaction on the quality of practice would be a *sine qua non*, provided for and valued by all parties, rather than a quid pro quo. It would also be a integral part of the preparation of teachers and required for continuation in their profession, and it would give them power. Teachers need capacity for this task.

## Mapping a Plan for Growth in Capacity: A Template

Educators have historically underestimated the challenge of the professional development process. The lack of a map or plan for growth in capacity for the South Vale staff while engaging in SBCDM may be typical of many attempts to implement change in schools. Therefore, it may be useful here to contrast the previous discussion of the efforts in SBCDM with the mapped events and capacity-building procedures that occurred in the process of reform of the mathematics program. For that endeavor, we faced the challenging task of transforming a generation of teachers who had been rote learners into functional constructivists—not just believers, but competent facilitators. And so, although we began in a familiar staff development way, we went beyond tradition and planned a map of much broader scope.

# Changing People: The Power of New Capacity

A metaphor may be applied to the process or map that I believe is necessary to bring teachers' capacity with new philosophies and methods to the point that they become natural and comfortable. The metaphor builds on the definitions of the construction of new knowledge that have been suggested by others. Living organisms that survive by consuming other organisms must first digest those organisms into absorbable and recognizable units (new perceptions must be connected to prior knowledge). Absorption of these units is a discriminating process; only desirable and safe units are normally absorbed (human goals control the learning process). The end of the process occurs when the units are reassembled or assimilated to become new parts or to replace old parts of the ingesting organism (accommodation or adaptation of prior knowledge).

On the basis of my experience with change and the incorporation of the ideas of those others mentioned above, I think this metaphor can be applied in a template for mapping a professional development program to increase teachers' capacity and power. The first stage of digestion and absorption of new ideas will be described here. Details of the assimilation stage will follow in Chapter 7. All steps require adequate time and the support of leadership!

## A Template for Increasing Capacity: Digesting and Absorbing

- Begin with reflective planning, listening to voices, and connecting prior knowledge and history to diagnosed needs (see Chapters 2 and 3).
- Introduce new perceptions: This may be a lecture or workshop as suggested by Joyce and Showers (1980). It may be connections to other places or systems or evocator-mediated peer reflections. It may need to be all of these and more.
- Develop a new consensus of goals.
- Provide the necessary tangible resources (e.g., books and other materials) and intangible resources (e.g., time and opportunities for further lecture and visits).
- Follow with practice and reflection in practice.
- Continue with research and peer reflections on practice.
- Enhance with monitoring (supportive leadership actions such as wandering around and asking questions), coaching, and feedback.

- Accompany the above with modeling.

Following this initial stage for digesting and absorbing new knowledge and practices must come the second stage of assimilation steps that assure ownership; make it part of the culture; make it comfortable, self-perpetuating, and refining; and bring the teacher the ultimate increase in power. I will present a template for the second stage in the following chapter.

## Applying the Template: Reflective Planning and Setting Goals

As described in preceding chapters, the original planning for the changes in South Vale's elementary math program began with a week-long immersion in research, reflection, and decision making by a volunteer group of 10 teachers. First, we looked at our own data, which revealed the nature of what was happening in our classrooms as well as the outcomes; discussed how it related to the national reports; and reviewed the observations that had been made in visits to schools with developmental math programs. Then we listened to the ideas of a guest speaker. This sequence is most important because a charismatic guest can prevent a group from careful listening and introspection.

This was all connected to our previous knowledge, particularly to our previous understanding of the work of Piaget (e.g., 1977). Although most of the elementary teachers were somewhat familiar with the Piagetian tasks and developmental levels, the data indicated that Piaget's work had little influence on instructional approach or curriculum.[2] It was this prior knowledge, however, that determined the planning cluster's goal that instruction should likewise proceed from the concrete to the abstract, with the use of manipulatives one prescription for increased reasoning and conceptual development. It was a good connection to a common history.

Less familiar to most of us was Piaget's concept that knowledge was self-constructed as a result of accommodations to new perceptions. We became aware of the recent revisions of constructivism that move away from the Piagetian notion that all children go through innately determined immutable stages (von Glasersfeld, 1990). Current constructivists place a great deal more emphasis on sociocultu-

## Changing People: The Power of New Capacity

ral mediations in the learning process (Vygotsky, 1978). Teachers are mediators, and this revision is empowering for them. As we addressed some of this, Elaine and the more informed special education teachers helped us to understand its significance. These were new perceptions, critical for the ownership of the new goals.

The planning cluster agreed on a set of goals and a rationale for change to meet them. The goals included some that were temporarily designed for the needs assessment, but the new set now represented our new perceptions and focused, much as the ensuing NCTM (1989b) standards did, on the need to prepare students to be capable problem solvers. We recognized that it was necessary to pay more attention to the development of reasoning skills and less to rote learning and computation. We would try to abandon absorption learning (the passive feeding of information or the "empty vessel" approach) and replace it with instruction that would help children construct their own concepts.[3] The group also agreed that students should have a positive attitude toward mathematics and confidence in their ability to learn. The decision to change was based on the recognition that the existing program did not include the complete spectrum of mathematical ideas, did not consider the different developmental levels and learning styles of students, did not allow for peer interactions, and did not account for the need to use concrete embodiments in the instructional process. We were not naive enough, however, to believe that just having or using manipulatives would accomplish our goals.

## Applying the Template: Providing Tangible Resources

The planning cluster unanimously recognized that we needed the support of new instructional materials and new instructional capacity to begin this reform. We considered several alternatives that we had seen others using in our visits and also heard a presentation about several different developmental math programs from a commercial textbook consultant. It would have been better, but probably an unrealistic challenge, for us to develop our own instructional materials; however, we had neither the capacity nor the time. Unfortunately, although the teachers were encouraged to try different programs and compare results, they all made the same choice after careful consideration of alternatives.

The cluster decided to pilot a commercially authored developmental math text that was used in Canada. This text was chosen because the teachers felt that they knew little about developmental mathematics and needed the structure that the text and the accompanying teacher's guide provided. Text-based programs are habitual crutches for elementary teachers, who are faced with the responsibility of planning for so many different subjects, and they often make uninformed and inappropriate choices. The danger of inflexibility is added when the text becomes too comfortable and is allowed to become the program instead of a resource for program (see Chapter 7). We were most fortunate in our choice, and the text and its supplementary materials (particularly the games) were critical as a beginning transition for the teachers, who had not learned mathematics with a focus on reasoning and had not been taught to teach this way. Most teachers need this type of support as they begin to develop their new capacities.

The true open-ended and creative discourse that encourages individually responsive alternate thinking and problem solving had to wait until we had more skill and supportive materials of our own. At the beginning, teachers stuck to the guide precisely. As they became more comfortable with the constructivist approach and cooperative learning, they began to design their own activities and dialogues. As I will describe ahead, the in-service workshops, disseminated literature, reflective meetings, modeling, and informal interactions with each other and with me were significant in building this capacity. In her fourth year of program implementation, Elaine revealed that she rarely used the teacher's guide anymore but understood why the newcomer next door needed it. Without the additional capacity-building activities, however, I doubt that the text itself would have really made a permanent difference.

Each teacher in the planning cluster became a piloting teacher and was given a generous budget to order the supportive manipulative materials. They perused catalogs and enthusiastically selected commercial materials. Although the guide offered suggestions for homemade materials, we were concerned that the burden of making them would be too great. Some rather uninformed and haphazard choices were made at this point, but this group of teachers felt especially rewarded by the opportunity to order instructional materials that no one else had. Teachers often value such materials highly, hoarding them and keeping them tightly bounded in their own classrooms. The effectiveness of some materials in the instructional process is debatable. Sometimes teachers do not use them well or use them at all. But there is no doubt in my mind that giving teachers materials—especially those of their own choosing—is motivating.[4] In the second stage of implementation, we again allowed teachers to choose materials, albeit from a more wisely chosen list. As I suggested in the preceding chapter, a leader who supplies tangible resources to teachers is providing support in the form of possibility.

## Applying the Template: Opportunity for Presentation With Practice

The planning cluster unanimously agreed that additional staff training was needed. After convincing Jim that some formal training was necessary and realizing our own limitations at that point, we decided to bring in outside experts. This was the traditional path of staff development, but it seemed like a good idea—especially because the piloting teachers asked for it, and it would be completely voluntary. The immediate need they perceived was for knowledgeable help in using the manipulatives to support the classroom discourse. Although the teacher's guide for the text was helpful, it was far from sufficient because the teachers had to reconstruct for themselves the mathematical concepts that they had learned by rote.

We were happy to find a pair of consultants who conducted a series of 10 after-school sessions for a total of 25 hours. The sessions were open to everyone who taught math, and teachers who participated were offered some credit toward salary increments. Thirty-three piloting and nonpiloting elementary and middle school staff members, representing approximately 50% of the eligible staff, attended these. In addition, the consultants conducted separate introductory formal all-day sessions for staggered groups of the entire elementary and middle school math staffs. These were scheduled on school days and required the use of substitute teachers. Formal workshops were also held for all of the teaching assistants.

The consultants were former elementary classroom teachers with recent doctoral degrees in curriculum and the experience and skill to relate well to the teachers. They modeled the use of the manipulatives, demonstrated good questioning skills, clearly justified the reasons for moving from a concrete experience to the abstract, and instructed the teachers to practice in pairs as they engaged in the exploratory discourse. Teachers were particularly interested in the motivating games that encouraged pattern recognition, helped develop skills, and structured social interactions.

The consultants' philosophy statement was appropriate—but there was something missing. It seemed as though the end toward which all of this was directed was merely to help the children reach a better understanding of the basic facts and algorithms. The importance of problem solving and self-constructed knowledge, although alluded to, was lost in the din of the materials. Where was reasoning and the acceptance of divergent thinking? What about the construction of concepts such as the part/whole relationships (Resnick, 1983) that were so prominent in the current research on how mathematical learning takes place? Wasn't it just as important for teachers to understand why the method was better as it was for them to learn how to use the new materials?

Not that the teachers objected—their interest was heightened more by the examples of games and activities than by the research or theory. Teachers are more likely to respond to the practical things that they can take with them immediately—and they did. The chip-trading games they laughed about as they played with each other soon ended up in their classes (and are still popular). Perhaps the games and manipulatives would have eventually allowed the teachers to construct their own new mathematical concepts, but this was an important cut at building the teachers' capacity and effecting a critical change—one that we could not afford to waste.

At each session of the in-service course, participants were therefore given articles from the journals and excerpts from the NCTM (1989b) standards, which provided some background theory. Some tension actually began to develop between the contracted consultants and me because of this agenda discrepancy. The teachers probably needed both agendas, but as usual there was a scramble for time and I had the power. Power is needed for control, but those who have power do not always exercise control well.

In the second year of implementation, a different consultant was more carefully chosen for a second round of in-service training that we hoped would attract the rest of the elementary teachers. Unfortunately, this in-service course was attended by only eight staff members, but they soon became competent and committed. Reflecting on recent experiences with parents and with formal in-service and pre-service teacher education, I have concluded that allowing adult learners to play with the manipulatives is critical. Like the children, adults may need to construct new meaning in this way, but they also benefit from interactive discourse with each other, with their students, and with their instructor and from the silent discourse a competent reader has with a competent writer. All must be orchestrated through adequate time.

I suggest that those contemplating using outside consultants spend careful time beforehand in specifying the desired outcomes and in setting the priorities clearly. In our case, it may have been a matter of chance that we were able to finally work out an after-the-fact compromise. Our consultants, moreover, had much that was needed to offer and in a form that none of us could at the time provide. This may not always happen. The evocator of change cannot completely delegate the professional development task to others whose visions or realities may not be the same. The evocator, however, must also be humble enough to listen, to learn, and to receive from others. The realities of the consensual domain are not inflexible.

## Applying the Template: Practicing, Researching, and Reflecting

"I can't believe how much time it takes to teach math this way. I just spent the whole morning on it. But it is working because the kids really understand what they are doing and they love math," Elaine reported as she began to use what we called at that time "the developmental approach" and the manipulative materials that accompanied it. The piloting cluster's initial reactions were mostly positive. Their direct role in the selection process and the resulting sense of ownership mitigated the discomforts of a new program. With much support from each other and their administrators, they pursued their challenge to change with vigor.

Concern arose, however, about the time consumed in preparing, distributing, and using manipulatives and in getting the children to conceptualize (see the discussion of the implementation dip in Chapter 8). The pace was definitely slower than in rote learning. These difficulties were to be expected. As with any new program, the teachers had no history to help them make the important decisions about what was absolutely necessary, what was optional, and what was probably unnecessary. They followed the teacher's guides religiously and struggled as they themselves began to understand some mathematical concepts for the first time.

The piloting teachers also began to set up the manipulative-based independent and cooperative learning activities that were suggested. The whole-class lessons were vastly different; math instruction time was more interactive with a minimal amount of written seat work. Pages of drill and practice materials were no longer used to control students while other things were happening. Sensing their needs, one principal assigned some extra teaching assistant time to each piloting teacher. The other principal was unable to do this, which may have caused some problems. We were also unable to follow through with this support for the following year—an unfortunate circumstance that should have been predicted. Change does require extra effort and energy on the part of every teacher who engages in it. Intangible resources such as teaching assistant time should be provided whenever possible, but they must be equitably offered or placed in a pool that teachers can control. Time as a whole is a resource that in the present structure of schools is severely limited (see Chapter 8).

Time and other forms of support came to the piloting teachers in several other ways. In addition to the in-service course in which they all participated, we met as a team for two full-day interactive problem-solving sessions. I also visited classes informally and volunteered to come in to trouble-shoot general problems and help diagnose individual student difficulties. Although a little of the usual administrator-teacher tension occurred, it diminished as we became a true collegial cluster, sharing and learning from each other. There was even a hint of jealously from the outsiders, but we offered to share materials when they were requested. The most significant reinforcement for teachers came from the children themselves, who looked forward to math and began to show the conceptual insights for which we had hoped. Their growing capacity encouraged us to learn more.

An example of the preceding is what Audra, a third-grade teacher at the time, and I discovered about students using manipulatives to learn how to solve problems involving subtraction. Audra, frustrated in her attempts to move the children from needing the manipulatives for the computations to being able to compute without them, asked for my help. I had no idea what the problem was, but we observed the children together and found that the way the children were using manipulatives was hampering their progress.[5]

## Changing People: The Power of New Capacity

Specific transitions are necessary between using manipulatives as concrete embodiments and abandoning them for symbolic representations. Whenever teachers are learning new approaches, they may encounter and be discouraged by difficulties such as these. As frequently happens, Audra had no history of learning or teaching this way on which to rely and had no text or guide to show her the way. She spent frustrating days with this problem before asking for help. Only careful clinical research found the source of the problem. In shared reflection about our findings, we generated a solution. Fortunately, Audra's support for gaining new capacity was not limited to the lecture or even to the lecture with practice of a formal in-service program.

We also met as a larger group in structured interaction sessions, which were held during the school day. At these sessions, we reflected as a collegial cluster on what we were doing and together solved some of the problems and gave each other courage to proceed. This bonding within the cluster was helpful the following year when we expanded the program to every K-4 classroom.

The pilot cluster agreed that the text program and guide were excellent but overwhelming in the demand for teacher preparation time. We made some decisions about how to be more selective of the text's recommended activities and spent time evaluating manipulatives and sharing ideas about their handling and distribution. We talked, for example, about Elaine's discovery that although at times teachers might need to have larger quantities of manipulatives, sharing between classes was possible: Once concepts were truly constructed by students using small numbers, the materials were not necessary except for introductory extensions—they actually became too cumbersome.

These sessions were also effective in clarifying and modifying our basic philosophy and provided further opportunities to share and explain some of the evolving research.[6] At these interactive feedback opportunities, we first reviewed the NCTM (1989b) standards, shared definitions and applications of constructivism, and considered the information-processing research. We soon developed a common vocabulary and began to plan the curriculum document I will discuss in Chapter 7. We also talked about how to answer parents' questions and planned the formative evaluation together. Genuine concern existed about the performance of the children on the CAT, even after a minor shift in the program sequence to help create a better alignment with the test was suggested. But the spirit of risk prevailed, and the teachers trusted themselves, their leadership, and what they were trying to accomplish.

Interactive follow-up reflective sessions such as these have been conducted with the series of peer coaches and their mentorees who participated in the recent summer institutes and workshops. The teachers came from different school districts and public and parochial schools, but the overarching outcome expressed was that the opportunity to reflect and plan with each other made the experience of change enlightening, gratifying, and less painful—in some respects, a joy.

## Applying the Template: Facilitating, Monitoring, Coaching, and Feedback

In the second year, when we were no longer dealing with volunteers, the teachers' discomfort that was caused by administrative pressure to proceed with the new program had to be mitigated. The overt resistance I discussed in Chapter 5 had ended, but some covert passive resistance from three or four teachers still remained. The evidence for it was in the unopened plastic bags of manipulatives and slipped-in ditto sheets of drill and practice. Almost all of this resistance was in the Birch Avenue School, which had the more mature staff and fewer original pilot teachers. In each case, the principals, the piloting peers, and I first exhorted on an intellectual level, assuming that the teachers' personal priorities were just to be the best.

Early in the school year, we provided an additional full-day workshop for everyone. The workshop was helpful, but it soon became apparent that we would have to do more. We tried to encourage everyone who had not participated in the first year's in-service program to enroll in the second year's after-school 15-hour course, but the response was disappointing (all of the reluctant teachers were already on maximum salary and were not interested in in-service credits). So a whole schedule of supportive activities during the school day was initiated. These activities were designed to help everyone, because even those who were enthusiastic were struggling with new vocabulary, new concepts, and new materials. The text program did not provide the important insights to help teachers understand why mathematics needed to be taught differently. Also evident were more of the specific conceptual transition problems with the manipulative materials, such as Audra's experience mentioned earlier.

The support system was intensive and structured and even included my presence in each school at regularly scheduled times, a programmed form of wandering around. There were many other examples of the supportive activities from Reitzug's (1994) facilitation and possibility categories, described in Chapter 5. Although it was a large investment for the school district, this support was necessary to help the teachers gain the capacity they needed to again feel comfortable and secure about what they were doing. Time for this became my high priority.

At first, my time was spent in reflective interactions with teachers and in informal modeling for individuals—sometimes at their invitation and sometimes following the principal's or my suggestion. Although a new hand delivered set of manipulatives seemed at the beginning to be a little gift or reward, the productive use of these materials required new skills and unpredicted energies on everyone's part. I often accompanied these materials with impromptu demonstrations of their use. This provided me with opportunities for informal monitoring, support, and clinical research.

Because not every teacher could have a teaching assistant and to reduce teachers' concerns about the threat to their control of students, the principals and I offered suggestions and materials to make the use of manipulatives more comfortable. For example, we provided each teacher with a rolling storage cart, individual bead frames for every child, and large Ziploc bags so that children could store loose materials at their desks. And quiet pom-poms were substituted for noisy beads and disks!

When teachers mentioned problems with individual students, they received some special help, sometimes in the classroom and sometimes in the remedial lab, usually in the presence of the teaching assistants who staffed it. What was discovered about the problems of individual students was then shared with their teachers. This often opened the door to constructive discourse with those who were less receptive. More articles were disseminated, and minigrants were offered to the more experienced original pilot teachers to model their lessons for other teachers. Working with small groups of children within the classroom and trouble-shooting with specific material and conceptual bugs also gave me the confidence to do some formal modeling.

No experts were available, so essentially I played the coaching role. My role as an administrator, however, also included an obligation as part of the traditional teacher evaluation process to observe the nontenured teachers and provide them with formal written feedback. This monitoring and feedback, when it is done properly, offers useful opportunities for capacity-building professional development. Later, some of these same teachers became coaches for newcomers. Tracing the substance of this coaching and feedback through these generations during a 5-year period demonstrates the value and impact of the process.

Although the observations were not in a strict clinical supervision mode (Cogan, 1973) because they also served contractual evaluation purposes, the climate of the pre- and postconferences was designed to provide for shared reflections. The written summaries documented these reflections and reinforced constructive approaches such as developing a lesson around problem solving, relating formal math to a student's informal experiences, using manipulatives, encouraging divergent answers, making mental computations and estimations, encouraging peer interactions, and aiming for concepts.

The summaries also established a new vocabulary for discourse and made connections between what was happening in the classroom and new ideas—often conceived as a result of personal reflections but also addressing the writings of others. The vocabulary is particularly important because it allows for efficient communication of the realities of the consensual domain. If a commonly agreed-on reality is that it is valuable for children to be able to make a judicious choice between counting on and counting down in solving subtraction problems, educators ourselves need to be clear in our communications that that is our aim. Below are excerpts from a written summary of reflections following an observation of Lila during the second year and corresponding reflections by Lila as she coached newcomers 5 years later.

*Year 2: Pearl as Coach for Lila*

> When someone volunteered the answer, you asked them to explain how the answer was arrived at. You also asked how other children had gotten the answer. Those who explained how they got their answers showed attainment of the cardinal principal—they knew that if you counted up to six that

meant there were six blocks there. They either used commutativity or counted on from four to ten. I don't believe anyone counted down from ten. This would have been a demonstration of their ability to make the "choice"—but counting down from ten with a subtrahend as large as four is very unusual. When you questioned them about the "whole" and the "parts," they seemed to be utilizing that developmental concept to help solve the problems. You continued with the blocks asking the children to make the shift to a difference between three and ten. While they were doing the problems, they wrote the symbols on their slates.

*Year 7: Lila as Coach for Andrea, Catherine, and Stephanie*

We also talked about the concept of subtraction as the part/part/whole and finding the difference between the part and the whole. . . . While the children were involved in this activity . . . we intervened when necessary to have them verbalize what they were doing.

I was presenting a lesson on "counting on." The children were encouraged to count by starting with the hidden number.

## Applying the Template: Modeling

When Lila coached, she did a great deal of modeling. Modeling is an effective method for developing new capacity. It is probably more effective than feedback from evaluative observations of teachers because it provides an opportunity for new perceptions without anxiety—although, in effect, it provides a subtle pressure to compete. At the beginning, I did most of the modeling. The evocator of change gains power and authority not just from position or appointment but in a professional culture, from personal credibility as well. It is easy for someone to tell others that their method is inadequate and they should try another. Sometimes that works, but sticking out your neck to prove that what you suggest does work is much more effective. I don't think I will ever try bungee jumping, but I certainly would like to see others succeed before I do.

The offer of minigrants to teachers who would do demonstrations for their colleagues was not an overwhelming success. The more experienced pilot teachers preferred to informally suggest ideas to the newcomers. Some of them, but not enough, accepted the challenge. Teachers are reluctant to appear as more expert than their peers, and they may see their colleagues as more competent critics. Sometimes this hesitance is overcome in a small collegial cluster that has grown from the informal culture. We had several examples of two or three teachers sharing lessons and providing each other with feedback during the second year, and later it became the standard for new teachers to be coached by the more experienced ones. Modeling was the favored approach to this.

As previously mentioned, the current endeavors with teachers from school districts other than South Vale employ peer coaching as a major component of the professional development process. In measurements of the elements of peer coaching (the different activities that teachers do together), teachers have identified peer modeling as one of the most common. When modeling was accompanied by peer reflection, it was the element most responsible for measured variance in the implementation of the specific changes sought (Solomon, 1995). Nevertheless, my position as an outside consultant in these instances precludes me from any control of the other variables that are discussed in this book, and I caution readers to understand that coaching and modeling are only pieces of the map.

In a collegial culture in which teachers themselves are the evocators of change, modeling for others may become less difficult. When an administrator, long out of the classroom, is the evocator, the task of modeling is challenging and only rarely attempted. It is not comfortable to go into a classroom with unfamiliar children and demonstrate a rusty craft that an audience of suspicious colleagues practices every day. The opportunity to convince others this way is, however, unmatched in its rewards. In our case, it proved that children could construct their own concepts and that unless they grasped for meaning, the learning was superficial.

At the beginning, some of the original piloting teachers and I modeled for individual teachers (see the example of Edith in Chapter 5), but we soon realized that demonstrations for single teachers were a valuable but inefficient use of time. The principals and I, therefore, arranged for groups of teachers to see model lessons. As part of the process, the observers were given written explications beforehand that called specific attention to the research-based reasons for each activity and asked the teachers to watch for the children's responses. The lessons clarified desired outcomes, demonstrated instructional mapping (scaffolding), and modeled feedback mechanisms. Every demonstration was followed by reflective discussions of the written material and the lessons.

The whole package of written explication, demonstration, and reflection provided an important capacity-building experience for all of us. Like the formal observations of teachers, they provided an opportunity for sharing new vocabulary and for practicing our own new discoveries and the suggestions of other researchers.

## Resistance, Constructivism, Capacity, and Power

For the few teachers (beside Greta) who were still passively resistant or unconvinced, I believe that modeling made a difference. Jane, a fourth-grade teacher who had been complaining about the time the new program took, observed a lesson in her colleague's class and then immediately tried the lesson with her own students. She called me that night and exclaimed, "They grabbed it, they really understood the concept of fractions, and so did I for the first time!" There was a thrill in her voice—the thrill of new power over her craft. She never complained about time again.

But evocators of change must face the reality that they can't win every skirmish. Demonstrations were arranged so that teachers who spent an unassigned period watching a model lesson in another class would be paid back with a model for their own class. Greta was the only one who didn't show up for her model observation, but when I volunteered to come in to her class to teach the children something, she gladly accepted. On the scheduled day, she called to tell me that she was home ill but asked if I would come while the substitute was there and teach her class anyway. She had missed the point completely, and I told her so.

Reflections on their own experience as learners and teachers are important decision determinants for teachers (Lortie, 1975). Greta had completely shut out the possibility that a single new experience might change her mind. Only careful research and reflection on the value of what she was doing in a changing environment would replace this opinion and her practice. But because she cared about her students, the measurement of her outcomes compared with those of her colleagues—and the changing attitudes of parents, who wanted more for their children—eventually provided the disequilibrium that helped Greta construct new knowledge and generate new goals for herself.

Constructivism posits that each of us constructs his or her own schemata: bits of knowledge, explanations, or pictures of reality stored in the brain—on the basis of their fit with personal goals, previously existing concepts, and new perceptions (von Glasersfeld, 1990). These pictures of reality may or may not be correct as judged by comparison with what most other human beings see as reality. Cobb (1990) ascribes the commonly held or shared realities to the "consensual domain" (p. 209). Knowing and agreeing with others that two and two is equal to four and that snow is white or without color are pictures of reality and constructions in the consensual domain. The instructional process then becomes a matter of helping the individual develop, confirm, or correct his or her own reality pictures to approach the realities of the consensual domain. Constructivists believe that learning does not take place until that newly formed construction of reality is put in place by the learner, and that learning does not occur when information is fed into a passive learner. The learner must take ownership. New knowledge must be digested, absorbed, and assimilated.

Increased capacity implies the ownership of new or adapted schemata. If the purpose of the teacher or the evocator is to change the capacity of others to represent his or her own vision and reality, then transferring that vision becomes a matter of helping the active learner form and take ownership of new constructions to share as a new consensual domain. All help does not necessarily have to come from the evocator; it can come from peers as well. Teachers individually engaged in reflective practice with new materials and ideas experience new perceptions and can construct their own new realities, values, and strategies. Teachers mutually engaged in reflection on action can help each other construct realities in response to new personal perceptions and those generated by the ideas of others. But in both cases, the ideas must fit goals and be evaluated in terms of previously held realities. They are selectively and slowly absorbed in varying and individualized ways through adequate time.

Providing teachers with the opportunities to build the selfconstructions that are required for new capacity is a complex time- and energy-consuming task for everyone—but worth the effort. New capacity for teachers will bring them new power because it will provide them with the rewards they value, the ability to reach their students, and the recognition that they have done so. In the chapter ahead, I will discuss how documenting outcomes with curriculum and then assessing them help new knowledge become assimilated and provide the measures that teachers need to realize these rewards.

## Notes

1. In a summer institute, a total of 74 experienced teacher mentors were trained to coach 1 to 4 mentorees. Year-long reflections from these mentors indicated that by the end of the school year, most of the peer interactions were mutually authoritative (Solomon, 1995).

2. Piaget's developmental levels have been interpreted by teachers as innate and immutable. His later ideas on the construction of knowledge are less well known and appreciated. Limiting understanding of Piagetian theory to recognition of the levels deprives teachers of a sense of power. If cognitive development is predetermined in their students, their role seems limited.

3. Self-construction by the students would in turn require connections between informal and formal experience, interactive discourse, acceptance of alternate solutions, use of manipulatives, and limitations of the focus on algorithms.

4. Manipulatives that represent real things are in themselves abstractions that require analogical connections. Teachers need to develop capacity in their use. They also need to learn when they may encumber new knowledge construction and when to discard them.

5. The children were using Diene's blocks (a place value manipulative sometimes called "powers of ten"), which forced them into an immature counting process that did not work easily in the algorithm. Together Audra and I planned an intermediate step in which we challenged the students with the blocks in front of them to predict the "difference" and move that first. This corresponded more closely to what needs to be done in the symbolic algorithm.

6. We talked about the work of Anderson (1990), who provided a more empirical rationale as well as a new vocabulary for making connections between formal school math and the children's informal knowledge. We also reviewed Resnick's (1983) ideas on mapping instruction and the various applications of the part/whole concept as mathematical applications of the ideas of the information processors and developed some benchmarks on the basis of Baroody's (1987) ideas on the learning to count sequence.

# 7

# Making It Your Own
*Assimilation and Reculturization*

### About This Chapter

Previous chapters have described how reflective practice in action, which is at the functional level of change, informs and fashions instruction by teachers in the dynamics of the classroom, and how reflections on action, when shared among peer groups, can increase teachers' capacity. Reflections by teachers are framed by their previous knowledge, experience, and values. Included in their values and standards, in addition to their own expectations, are the documentations of the written curriculum and the expectations of externally designed assessments.

This chapter begins with some perspectives on the nature of school curriculum and its relationship to the process of school change, followed by an explanation of how curriculum has been controlled by the power of standardized and state-mandated tests and/or textbook-bound alternatives that set culture-embedded standards—standards that limit teachers' abilities to respond flexibly to changes or differences in their students and their environments. I then propose a template for directing that power into consensually developed content contracts or standards that are matched to long-term, teacher-generated assessments, which have the flexibility to respond to the variations in the teaching-learning experience and also offer some degree of equity in expectation. Last, I will illustrate how such documentation can bring teachers to the assimilation and ownership stage of the building of new capacity and suggest how sharing it with stakeholder parents can complete reculturization.

## Where Does Curriculum and Assessment Fit?

As I have previously noted and as Sarason (1990) predicted, recognition is emerging that the restructuring of school management systems does not automatically lead to a change in culture or to the improvement of student performance. McNeil and McNeil (1994) have most recently explained this by classifying shared decision making as an organizational rather than an educational change. They have suggested that school decisionmakers place a lens on the educational change, rather than on the whole business of managing schools. I agree with their suggestion—especially in light of experience with the limited energy resources of teacher-leaders—but cannot lose sight of the evidence that organizational and educational changes are interdependent and can be mutually supportive if they share the common thread of collegiality.

Like the McNeils, Fullan (1994) believes that a focus on desired educational goals and content is essential. He makes a similar distinction between *restructuring* and *reculturization* and cautions against the mandated involvement of teachers in site-based decision making if they are from cultures in which collegiality is far from the norm and in conflict with their personal history and imperatives. Fullan recommends that schools consider the change process as complex, involving simultaneous influences and actions. He uses a metaphor of interlocking gears and cogs to describe a framework for linking classroom and school improvement (see Fullan et al., 1990).

Interlocked within Fullan's gear of classroom improvement are the cogs of content, instructional strategies, and skills. Together, by most current definitions, these inextricably interdependent components form the curriculum. This differs from the more traditional view that considers the term *curriculum* to imply the content and separates it from *instruction*, which implies the strategies and environment. I agree with the current view of the relationship but will use the term *content* to distinguish it from the strategies and environ-

# Making It Your Own

ment because of my belief that the degree of individual teacher autonomy that is realistic and desirable may be different for these components of curriculum. The specific nature of a proposed change is also directly related to its acceptability. In general, teachers are less receptive to changes in their roles or to organizational change than they are to traditional changes in curriculum (Solomon, 1977).

Although the process of assessment, too, is sometimes considered separately, it may be more significantly and holistically viewed in its relationship to the components of the curriculum. They come together in the actions of reflective practice. In the dynamics of the classroom, the teacher constantly assesses the students and his or her actions in terms of the habits, values, and contracts of the curriculum and frequently makes almost immediate adjustments in content or strategy. Long-term reflections on practice can be in response to more carefully planned assessments, valuable to the individual teacher and to other stakeholders. These assessments are best if they are matched to curriculum and meet consensual standards.

Most of the past literature on the change process refers to the phase in which a given change becomes part of the culture as *institutionalization*—a rather cold and formal word. In relationship to the school as a system, I prefer Fullan's term, *reculturization*, because it recognizes the power of the underlying informal culture. In the previous chapter, I suggested a metaphor of digestion, absorption, and assimilation for the individual teacher who forms that culture and must gain new capacity. The assimilation stage makes a new idea or method a habit of practice—one that feels comfortable, brings satisfaction and reward, and creates ownership.

Ultimate ownership of a new idea may require documentation. For educators, the form of this documentation is the written curriculum and assessments. For curriculum to have the greatest meaning to you as an individual teacher, you may first need to say it, write it in your own words, and confirm it with your students and perhaps with your peers; then you may want to measure your accomplishment of it on your terms or as it has meaning to you and your students. For curriculum to have meaning for a culture, other stakeholders must be considered and contracts made or consensus reached. But those contracts need only be for the content outcomes to be achieved. Individual teachers need the power and freedom to respond creatively to their situation-bound exigencies.

## What Is the Present Status of Curriculum?

Most people have seen those Russian dolls that sit one inside another. They get smaller and smaller, but the littlest one is just a miniature of the one on the outside. If educators think about the existing curriculum of schools that way, we would probably agree that the outermost layers are pretty much the same. Most schools in this country have similar general content goals for their students, and they have been that way for a while. Despite many minor and major attempts at renewal, little real change has occurred during the past in the outside form of curriculum content. Historically, in response to external pressure, school curriculum gets dressed with new embellishments. But its basic outer form hardly changes, although the child and the learned curriculum on the inside vary from moment to moment.

New knowledge of history, technology and science, and recurring fashions such as career education are added on to the existing forms with little attention to growing bulk. Longstreet and Shane (1993) describe it as "wanting it all" and "wanting it the way it was" (p. 94). Even most of the recent technology changes have been adaptations of habits of practice (e.g., computer software that is essentially drill and practice). The rare occasion when the outside content has been really different often creates great controversy. The addition of curriculum dealing with AIDS is an example.

Nevertheless, as we get deeper and deeper inside to the levels that represent the taught content and strategies of individual classrooms, the representations are increasingly different: different from each other and different from the outermost layer. In its present state, most curriculum is rarely structured with continuity of design toward purpose. And when we finally reach the innermost layer of the children who are the individual learners, we find them quite different from each other and different from what they were not too long ago. English and Steffy (1982) and others have made distinctions between the written, taught, tested, and learned curriculums and have noted the corresponding gaps between what is supposed to be taught, what is taught, and what is really learned and measured.

The Russian dolls are duplicates that fit snugly inside each other. Few connections and controls lie between the disparate layers of the school curriculum; they fit loosely within each other. This partially

# Making It Your Own

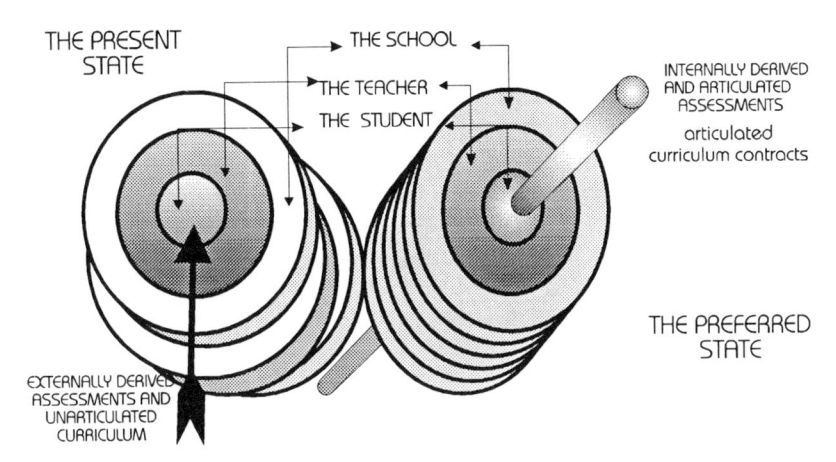

**Figure 7.1.** Eliminating the Discontinuities: Connecting Curriculum and Assessment

explains why many changes in the public outside layer, which is the most subject to political pressure, only minimally affect the innermost layers that really make a difference. The inner layers are unconnected, more private, and the most resistant. Because of these discontinuities, there are separate external efforts to control the inner layers. Examples of these controls are standardized tests and texts, which, unfortunately, look much like each other as they try to control the distinct layers within. Traditional administrative leadership also makes its attempt to control the disparate manifestations of a seemingly common curriculum purpose, but as I have previously discussed, the leadership is often inconsistent and locked in a struggle for power.

Glatthorn (1987) recognizes that the gaps in curriculum may be because of what he calls the organic curriculum, the nondocumented curriculum that arises in the situation-bound environment of the classroom. He considers this organic curriculum of value but also recognizes that individual teachers cannot have complete autonomy and suggests a consensual mastery curriculum that is the goal or standard for everyone. The United States already has a mastery curriculum that is molded and documented by standardized tests, but it may not be consensual or designed to achieve equity or encourage creative teaching. Transforming the tests may be a solution.

## The Power of Tests

Resnick (1992), who helped with many understandings in the mathematics changes at South Vale, has launched a major plan to change the mastery curriculum in a number of content areas on a national scale. The way to do this, she believes, is to begin by changing the standardized tests because of the evidence that these determine what teachers teach. Resnick and Resnick (1989) offer the following principles and advice:

> You get what you assess (teachers will teach to tests).
> You do not get what you do not assess (what is not tested is not taught).
> Build assessments toward which you want educators to teach.
> By placing curriculum at the heart of testing decisions these principles assert that tests must be chosen directly from it, and thereby promote the goals considered most central and important in education. (p. 66)

Wiggins (1989b) agrees with the foregoing and proposes the use of "authentic tests" that give "evidence of knowing," are "central to instruction," and reveal to the "test-taker the actual challenges and standards of the field." Wiggins flouts existing standardized tests for their concentration on thoughtless short-term recall, their lack of evaluation of "habits of the mind," and their inability to be of "constructive use to further knowledge" (pp. 704-706). This relates to my suggestion in the template below for recursive in-tandem review of content and assessments. Wiggins also attributes the lack of authentic tests to the failure of schools to appropriate funds for the purpose of developing such instruments and links (as do I) redesign of testing to the restructuring of schools.

Like Resnick, Wiggins (1989a) also suggests that "we design and then teach to standard setting tests so that practicing for and taking the tests actually enhances rather than impedes education" (p. 41). They both agree that to achieve equity, the same standards should exist for all students. This is an attempt to bring about change in the inner curriculum layers by changing the controlling assessments.

As long as these assessments evaluate only the broad-based common goals and standards, they sound like a good idea. My concern with this approach, however, is the danger of putting too much emphasis on them and not enough on the connections between layers and on the sharing and consensus reaching at the inner layers

# Making It Your Own 141

that are closer to the child. I also believe that no matter how "authentic" tests are, if they are improperly used, test controls at the outermost layer can encumber the ability to respond dynamically to the individual nature of the teacher and the child.

The goal of equity is worthy, and the potential of common standards and assessments as a means to reach that goal is reasonable. My experience, however, indicates that tests and standards would be best if they were determined only broadly from the outside in by a spectrum of stakeholders (parents, students, community, and national decision makers) and designed more specifically from the inside out by peer groups of those who carry out the function of education: classroom teachers. If, like the east and west branches of the railroad, they all connect, then a good chance for improvement exists. Better connections between the layers of content and assessment are needed the most.

South Vale teachers' comfort with their new mathematics program was originally derailed by their anxiety over its congruence with the nationally standardized CAT. Cheryl, a third-grade teacher, was concerned about how her students performed on this test. She saw the test as the priority and explained, "I needed to stop the manipulatives so that I could drill my class for the Californias." Her principal, Meg, and I reassured her with a promise: "You will not be held accountable for any decrease in scores as we make the transition to less drill and practice, more reasoning, and our own criterion-referenced tests. Tell the parents who are concerned to call us."

Finally, we tried to help Cheryl and many of the others by abandoning the computation part of these tests altogether. But it wasn't until she had, on her own, given students the suspended computation test that she was convinced that the new methods she struggled with had worked. Students explained their correct answers on untaught algorithms: "We estimated and chose the closest answer." Estimation had become an embedded and valuable skill in their problem-solving repertoire, but it was not specifically tested.

The CAT was designed to test textbook objectives commonly used in this country during the 1980s and therefore was not a true indicator of the success of the new program at South Vale. It was, however, a measure of personal achievement for the teachers—even though they complained. Tests have power over teachers because of the feedback they provide. In some cases, teachers may need (and desire) that feedback to confirm the value of their efforts. In other cases, in which tests are used by others to measure and control teachers, tests can also be destructive to teacher and student. For example, a large-scale analysis of time spent on preparation for standardized tests revealed that the teachers of classes with high percentages of minority students spent significantly more time in preparation (Madaus et al., 1992). Their entire curriculum is driven and limited by the tests.

Just as we cannot afford to base educational endeavor on anachronistic instructional methods and irrelevant content, we must avoid succumbing to the strangulating power of externally imposed, unaligned, and closed-ended tests. The South Vale High School curriculum was tightly controlled by the Regents exams. The evidence of their power over teachers was clearly demonstrated in teachers' anxiety about the results. This was most obvious in the math and science classes, in which the tests could be directly connected to one year's experience with the same teacher. The written state curriculum and old exams drove the day-to-day curriculum decisions with intensity. Even the texts were chosen on the basis of their match with the Regents exams and were frequently of low quality. In the English and social studies classes, in which the exams were comprehensive and covered several years of content, this connection was somewhat diminished but still evident in the selection of texts.

The power base of the New York State Education Department had always been manifested in its testing program. Its power had grown even stronger in the previous decade of emphasis on "back to basics" with the additions of an extensive mandated competency testing program at every level. These tests were also connected to the state's widened role in the implementation of federal regulations to protect persons with disabilities and in the management of programs supported by federal funds.

An annual comprehensive assessment report by the state gave the results of this testing both to the local district and to the local press. Districts responded with public hearings, presenting these results along with other standardized test results. The whole process intensified the emphasis on formal testing. Only within the last few years, with its *New Compact for Learning* (University of the State of New York, 1991), has the New York State Education Department evidenced a willingness to relinquish some of its centralized authority over curriculum and assessment. A recent document suggests that it will provide "top-down support for bottom-up reform" (Uni-

# Making It Your Own 143

versity of the State of New York, 1994, p. 1). It even proposes wide local choice in its state-managed testing program and more authentic portfolio pieces designed at both the state and local levels. The state has not, however, abandoned its power. It is already experimenting with a school inspection system (patterned after European models) to replace testing.

For South Vale elementary teachers, the relatively easy competency tests seemed less controlling than the CAT. The competency tests were administered only at benchmark levels: at the third and sixth grade for mathematics and reading and once each at other grade levels for science, social studies, and writing. The CAT was given at every grade level and results were examined by parents and the community on a yearly basis. Like the comprehensive exams at the high school, benchmark tests are less clearly attributable to a specific teacher and more indicative of system strength.

Testing programs can easily function as prodders of change, but they can just as readily serve as dysfunctional impediments if they are not aligned with changing curriculum and if teachers become anxious about possible diminutions in their students' performance. Evidence of this came at South Vale in the lower level of anxiety about the almost simultaneous change in the science program, in which formal testing was limited to the benchmark fourth grade and responsibility was diffused. There was much less resistance to the new science program for other reasons as well (e.g., student control factors and a long history of similar programs), but for the changes in math, the CAT was a palpable restraining force. Why should teachers bother learning a new approach if the test evaluated an old one?

Nevertheless, when the results proved positive, it was comforting to realize that, whatever the CAT tested, the students succeeded despite the new approach. Definitely needed, however, was an instrument that would indicate whether the desired new outcomes were also achieved.[1]

## The Hegemony of Texts

Texts are the backbone of the American school curriculum. In many cases, they *are* the curriculum. In the South Vale High School courses in which the state Regents tests were not given, the taught curriculum was most frequently based on a textbook and less frequently on a locally developed written curriculum that the teachers themselves had been involved in writing—but this was usually attached to a particular text. At the elementary level, the content was so driven by the texts that some teachers did not even know that written state curriculum guides existed. Occasionally, they used some activity curriculum units that they had been involved in writing, but most often they followed the same texts and teacher's guides and were under constant pressure to cover the material in them.

The new elementary science program that articulated with the state curriculum did not have a traditional text. The curriculum objectives and matching activities had been developed by teachers on statewide teams and was a process approach that was patterned on the highly successful Science Curriculum Improvement Study (SCIS) program that it replaced, but it did not have comparable quality.[2] The South Vale teachers had therefore made some adaptations and added a selection of supporting trade books. The program also came with a test-based management system that the teachers fortunately did not use.

Some teachers and parents who were not comfortable with science processes would have preferred a text, but in an example of the power of consistent leadership, elementary principals and I had successfully lobbied against elementary science textbooks for 23 years because we could not find one that was appropriate. We knew that in their presence, elementary teachers might slip comfortably into the text as the curriculum and neglect the important science processes. The trade books that replaced them were purchased in class sets and keyed to the hands-on discovery activities. Teachers made their own choices of these books and were encouraged to share them with their colleagues.

In a biting criticism of school texts, Tyson-Bernstein (1988) accuses texts of the following:

> They take on too many topics and treat them superficially; there are too many unexplained facts, and there is not enough context; new knowledge is more often piled on than assimilated; the prose is dumbed down to accommodate the poorer reading skills; faddist and special-interest group messages, however meritorious, appear as bulges or snippets of content; flashy graphics and white space further compress the already compressed text; instructors (and teachers) are se-

duced by, and addicted to, teacher manuals and ancillary products that promise to take the work (and the judgment) out of teaching. (p. 194)

Tyson-Bernstein's (1988) remedy for this calls for a starting point that looks first at the curriculum, which is overloaded and lends itself for an emphasis on coverage rather than coherence, interest, and depth. She places the major responsibility for improvement of texts on the shoulders of the academy—the college professors who write them—but also suggests that public schools need to resist "fads and pressures" (p. 195). I believe that schools also need to remove textbooks from their role as curriculum contracts and replace them with documents that reflect consensus on what is important to the layers closest to the child.

Textbooks are a powerful part of school cultures and can become the drivers of change or can militate against it. The publication of textbooks is a major business that responds to market demands. If the market demands different choices, business will respond. Textbooks' quality, articulation with goals, and role as a resource in each individual situation are important considerations in any change process. At South Vale, we needed and used a well-developed text that matched our goals to help us get started on our elementary math changes, but soon we also needed a curriculum contract.

## Getting It All Together

The trick is to harness the traditional power of tests and texts and redirect it toward productive change and self-generated renewal. Attempts at change must consider the entrenchment of present practice and the nature of educators and school cultures. If texts offer comfort to teachers, schools cannot discard them without appropriate substitutes but should use them as resources, not as contracts, and should choose them wisely. If teachers and the public need the feedback of tests, then tests should match the curriculum and help direct the teachers' endeavors. And, using the aforementioned definitions by Wiggins (1989a, 1989b), tests should be authentic. Clarity and consensus of purpose in a written content contract is a good beginning.

Documents such as the NCTM standards (1989b), *America 2000: An Education Strategy* (U.S. Department of Education, 1990), and *2061: Science for All Americans* (American Association for the Advancement of Science, 1989) are not consensual contracts and, thankfully, are not mandates. They are worthy and useful models or guidelines that represent some of the best thinking in this country about what is important and offer promise as the basis for contracts. Following its own *New Compact for Learning* (University of the State of New York, 1991) and using the above documents as models, the state education department recently published more specific curriculum frameworks as guides for the development of local curriculum standards. Other states have issued similar documents.

The mandate in New York requires that these local standards be responsive to a clearly communicated vision shared by a variety of stakeholders including teachers, parents, students, and the community at large. This requires reculturization and will not be an easy task. If properly implemented, the process of redocumenting the frameworks into written contracts that represent a consensus and meet local needs may be helpful.

## Reaching Consensus

When ideas are discussed orally, their power is restricted by their ability at the moment to help the conversants construct new knowledge. When ideas are committed to writing, their power has longevity, and consensus is harder to reach. On the basis of my many opportunities to write curriculum or supervise the writing and implementation by others and my most recent experiences preparing teachers to lead others in the process, I offer the following observations.

- The most used curriculum documents are teacher generated, but there is little real dissemination beyond the writing group. The level of implementation varies indirectly with the distance of the teacher from the writing source.
- Teacher-generated curriculum is most original in its choices of activities. These are much easier for teachers to write than outcomes. Outcomes or performance objectives tend to be hand-me-downs or to be scavenged from other sources (this is even true of teachers writing individual education plans for special education students). Because the outcomes are not original, they get little attention, and teachers focus more on the activities.
- Most curriculum documents are syntheses or adaptations of others. They rely heavily on state-generated frameworks or

# Making It Your Own

textbooks for their objectives. The experts who write the latter are often too isolated from the teachers who use them.
- Teachers can become experts at writing curriculum outcomes or standards; they need experience, guidance, and time.
- The greatest value of written curriculum is accrued by the writer in the process of writing, but with consensus and quality, there will be benefits for many.
- Consensus may be necessary only at the outcome or standard level. Teachers flourish when they are encouraged to be innovative and flexible in the way they choose materials and activities and are given the time and other resources to do this.
- Most parents do not believe that they have the expertise to write curriculum and defer to teachers as the experts.[3] But their voices need to be heard.

Preceding chapters have made many suggestions for preparation for change and increasing teachers' capacity to implement new ideas and methods. Considering the preceding observations, I now offer the following template for assimilating new practices and making them part of the culture. When you have committed yourself to something in writing, you own it. In the case of the changes in mathematics program in South Vale, documentation did not occur at the start, but we were dealing with something new and different. It may be possible to redocument present practice at an earlier point.

## A Template for Assimilation and Reculturization

The following template represents a plan for the documentations of the assimilation stage of increased capacity (people change) and follows the first stage as described in Chapter 6. It assumes previous opportunities and time for adaptation and personalization of new instructional methods, environments, and/or purposes (digestion and absorption). It also assumes prior consideration of the school community's history, visions, and voices and presupposes leadership as discussed in prior chapters. It does not include the generation of activities and other resources. Teachers need more autonomy over these. Activities should be individually developed or, preferably, created by interacting peer teams. For final reculturization, the documents will require publication and sharing with other stakeholders, students, and parents. The steps include these:

1. *Make some critical choices.* You can't do it all, and it is not necessary to contract with a written document for everything. Listen to the voices and make some critical decisions about what needs uniformity and coherence and what needs greater autonomy.

2. *Put it into your own words.* Proximal (face-to-face) peer groups of teachers, working alone or with other stakeholders, should paraphrase any externally created, inherited, or internally created but distal documentations (e.g., professional group standards, state curriculum guides, text-based programs, or even documents produced by teacher committees) into newly generated consensual and written contracts that agree on general outcomes or content standards. Little of such content is originally created from scratch, but if it is necessary to do this, more time needs to be allocated and some expertise may be required.

3. *Agree on measures.* Once the content standards are agreed on, the peer groups of teachers should also decide on what matching long-term group measures or assessments to use. These may be externally produced, but they are best if they are internally written by teachers and authentic as described above. Their interpretations must, however, be understandable to the variety of stakeholders. Decisions should also be made on the nature of publication and sharing of the results of these measures.

4. *Review results and redesign recursively.* Each administration of the measures should be followed by a peer review of the results, the assessment instruments, and the content standards and by the sharing of new research findings and suggestions for possible effective strategies. The written curriculum needs to be metamorphosing and flexible but identifiable and used.

5. *Publish and disseminate the documents and results.* Parents need to be involved as much as possible in the development of the content document and informed of the assessment results. Schools may need to actively increase parents' capacity to understand the documents and results.

## Why Local Documentation of Curriculum Is Needed: An Example

When we began to implement mathematics changes at the elementary level in South Vale, the standards were only broadly stated

# Making It Your Own

as final goals. In the second year of implementation, we recognized that we needed an assessment of our own, one that evaluated our program. This made us realize the need for a documented curriculum. We had been addressing our general goals and reflecting constantly on what we were doing, researching solutions to our problems, and absorbing the findings of others, but essentially the only specifically written curriculum was our text program and a mostly unused and outdated state curriculum guide.

To accomplish our goals, we needed the greater capacity that more specific curriculum and assessments would bring. To reflect on the progress of our journey and see if we were on the right road, we needed to clarify priorities and to identify and mark the benchmarks and checkpoints.

Although the development of competence is unique to the individual and dependent on the nature of instruction with its accompanying social interactions and resources, certain common conceptual (what you know) and procedural (what you can do) cognitions are required to become successful survivors in modern societies. Perhaps these cognitions represent the consensual domain described by Cobb (1990). They are the constructions of knowledge that allow people to communicate with each other. These cognitions can form the framework for intermediate outcome goals or benchmarks.

The knowledge base of these cognitions in elementary math—especially the conceptual ones—and the ability to assess them were limited because, in most cases, they have not been defined (Carpenter, Fennema, Peterson, & Carey, 1988). Most objectives stated in math curriculum and texts and tested by standardized tests are merely subdivisions of traditional computation skills written mostly as decomposed procedural objectives (Wood & Cobb, 1990). For example, they usually read "students will be able to do or perform [an algorithm]," and rarely, if ever, "students will understand how the part/whole relationship applies to solving problems that require addition or subtraction."

How could teachers aim for cognitions when they were not clear on what they were? The available documents were an iteration of the rote procedures they had learned. What our math program was addressing had never been documented—at least not in the form we needed. Some recent tests require knowledge of concepts with their problem-solving questions, but the concepts are embedded, not explicitly stated. Nor was there a realistic explanation of the developmental sequences, interactions, and transitional microstages that would help teachers lead students to the constructions of the consensual domain.[4] We needed to come to our own consensus on these concepts, and we needed to decide on a sequence and grade level expectations that would help us design matching assessments.

### Making Choices and Putting Them Into Your Own Words: Needing Help

We had many pieces to consider for the first steps of the documentation tasks. The teachers were using a text that almost everyone liked; we had a state curriculum guide and were bound by its matching tests; we had our new knowledge of how children learn and a new appreciation for self-constructed and divergent thinking; we had a new set of goals for the new era of technology; and we had new manipulative materials. The curriculum needed to be eclectic, considering the needs of the child, the content, and society. Making choices and putting them into our own words was a great challenge, and there was so little time!

It is wise to start by eliminating what isn't necessary. Our reflections suggested no need for documenting activities. The text program and the many ideas that teachers had shared in reflective meetings or had gleaned from the in-service program and modeling gave them much with which to work. Many other creative things were going on. We could concentrate on a set of concepts and procedural outcomes with a sequence map that articulated our own goals with the state's standards, a map that would help us plan and trace our progress. For this, we needed our own matched assessments.

The role of the expert in curriculum change has to be carefully orchestrated. It's like walking on glass. If a person steps too hard, he or she destroys teacher agency and the purpose gets hurt in return. In a perceptive analysis of teacher agency in the process of curriculum change, Parris (1993) argues convincingly for greater teacher autonomy over curriculum. She describes how four teachers adapted a word processing curriculum, which was developed by two of their more computer-knowledgeable colleagues, according to their own needs, skills, and interests. Each paraphrased differently and used the curriculum in disparate ways, but they used it, and the students benefited. The curriculum contract that students would use word processing in their writing was met, although there was teacher agency in the specifics of the implementation.

Parris (1993) concedes, however, that the teachers she observed depended on the expertise of their colleagues, which they did not have, to get change started. In the South Vale case, my own impatience took over. I may have made a mistake by taking on the expert's role, assuming responsibility for the concepts and matching procedures in the first part of this documentation—a scope and sequence covering grades K-4. It would have been better if each of the teachers had generated the concepts in his or her own words, but realistically, this was hardly possible without the benefit of a great deal of research and instruction. It was the teachers' best judgment, however, that determined the final sequence.

The teachers were trying to change! But most of them were still struggling to implement the new ideas in cookbook fashion as they sacrificed their ditto sheets for hands-on manipulatives and reasoning. Dog-eared teacher's guides were evidence of this. How could we ask them to go one step further—to creatively predict the concepts their students would need to solve problems? Even mathematical researchers are still struggling with the concepts and terms. Nevertheless, I am confident that with a collegial culture that supports shared reflection and informed renewal, in time, teachers' capacity can grow enough to enable them to be ever more successful at predicting and then promoting the development of critical concepts. Preliminary affirmation of this is that using the K-4 scope and sequence as a guide, teachers produced their own assessment instruments on the basis of the concepts and procedures and, in the process, made many suggestions for revisions. And middle school teachers (with minor help from me) extended the scope and sequence through the eighth grade.

The construction of this new scope and sequence of standards was complex. At the reflective meetings, the teachers and I had frequently discussed the articulation of the text with the state curriculum and with research findings on how children learned. We had identified some matches, discrepancies, and omissions. Then Elaine, Lila, and the other pilot teachers searched the text for further concept statements that would inform us of what our benchmarks should be. Although we found some in the text, my own critical analyses of the questions on the CAT and state tests, in which conceptual outcomes were implied in the procedures that were required, and the current research were much more fruitful.[5] Listening directly and closely to students' verbalizations at different grade levels, which showed how the students were thinking, and the teachers' reports of coverage, successes, and frustrations helped us to determine the sequence.

The state curriculum guide was a starting point for a first draft set of concepts, which were matched to desired outcomes or standards. These were expressed in the form of procedures and designated as assessment criteria. The concepts and criteria were arranged in topical categories across the K-4 grades. On the basis of all of the feedback, suggested median expectations were attached to a spread of three grade levels. Although this scope and sequence clearly documented what we needed to reach for, there were no hard-and-fast rules for how to get there, and there was developmental leeway in the expectation levels. Teachers were encouraging the children to think divergently and needed to be offered the same challenge.

In appreciation of the need to consider history and prior knowledge, the final design of the math document tried to help teachers make the transition from the familiar, traditional form of objectives to a new set of outcomes or performance standards. The scope and sequence began with titles that were the customary decomposed procedural objectives as they related to algorithmic procedures, but these were then connected to the new standards that focused on understanding, problem solving, and reasoning and were grounded in a matched set of clearly stated concepts.

Although sketches of parts of the concept list were shared with teachers at various stages and they made many corrections and suggestions, the immediate reaction of the elementary staff when they saw the complete draft of the document was anxiety. They were overwhelmed by its breadth, although the titles were all in their text objectives and the state curriculum guide and most of the concepts were already familiar to them because of professional development efforts. They had never seen a curriculum framework in this form, across grade levels and matched to concepts and outcomes.

Many teachers who were procedural learners had never thought of mathematics conceptually. Others used these concepts subliminally but had never seen them stated. Some disclaimed ownership— a predictable and reasonable reaction because they had not yet had the personal opportunity to paraphrase; they had not contracted for this document. They would, however, soon have that opportunity as they constructed their own assessments and reviewed results.

## Agreeing on Measures

Evaluation of the new elementary program was truly complex. We were not just implementing a new text or instructional device. We had become involved in a basic paradigm shift from absorption theory, with its passive receiver and externally controlled associative, accumulative, and uniform learning approach, to cognitive theory, with its focus on relationships, active construction of knowledge, and recognition that true learning must be internal (Baroody, 1987).

Paper-and-pencil formal tests are limited in their ability to evaluate accomplishment of such a paradigm; the more authentic evaluations in our day-to-day reflective search for feedback were more appropriate. But we needed to demonstrate public accountability and substitute something for the inadequate CAT. We may have also needed the public pat on the back that such an assessment might bring.

Soon after they received the scope and sequence, elementary teachers were asked to consider the assessment criteria and the median expectations for their own levels, to estimate how much they expected to accomplish by the testing date, and to write questions for a criterion-referenced test on the basis of this estimate. The challenge of writing test questions was daunting. Elementary teachers rarely write evaluative items. More often, these are selected from workbooks, texts, or standardized tests. Despite all the preparation and their own expressed need for something of their own, the task of preparing a test—even with the scope and sequence and assessment criteria carefully outlined—was both threatening and formidable.

They were each asked to submit only seven questions but were encouraged to work with their colleagues to avoid duplication and to facilitate consensus. "We don't have the time," they complained to me. "Why don't you do it?" That would have been a serious mistake; they needed to put the outcomes into their own words, and writing assessment items would help them do it. It would also require them to really take stock of what they had accomplished—and the results could not easily be cast aside as unrelated to their own programs. They needed time and support to help them prepare the questions, however. The principals helped by providing meeting time for this, and I spent time in the schools explaining the task.

A cluster representing both elementary schools and each grade level then met with me to select the questions. Everyone's lack of experience was obvious in the failure of some questions to match the outcome criteria as they were explicitly stated in the scope and sequence and in the struggle for appropriate directions and form. It was also obvious, as previously mentioned, that some conceptual outcomes could not be evaluated by paper-and-pencil tests. We would need other forms of assessment.

When they first saw the duplicated tests, teachers again expressed anxiety. The form was different, there were many diagrams, and the tests did not have the polish of their printed commercial tests. Some of problems were presented in noncanonical form (to evaluate understanding). The tests had no time limits, and children had the option to use manipulatives if they needed them, but, as expected, change is discomfiting—even when it is generated at close range.

In any case, the teachers' endeavors and concerns helped to focus on the connections between content and assessment, and we had a beginning contract. The scope and sequence with its component concepts and the assessments were only working drafts, subject to constant future revisions as we learned more, but it gave us a documented start. The first major revisions actually were made immediately after development in the following summer and fall, when teachers met in grade level workshops with me to review results of the tests.

## Reviewing Results and Redesigning Recursively

We had embedded the tests in a computer-based, in-house management system that provided class mastery reports for each teacher as well as individual student mastery reports to pass on to the next year's teacher. In the workshops, the teachers and I looked at the reports, checked the tests carefully to see how they were related to the scope and sequence's conceptual objectives, and discussed how to change the contract documents of content and assessment.

Ownership grew as the discourse concentrated on reaching consensus about the grade level expectations, as the conceptual vocabulary became more familiar, as examples of possible learning experiences were shared, and as teachers identified omissions that were promptly incorporated into the document. But most important, we considered ways to improve our strategies for the coming year. For the next few years, these workshops were repeated annually, and revisions in the documents were made.

# Making It Your Own

The sessions proved to be a critical benchmark in reculturization. Our new assessments replaced the CAT as the teachers' criteria for success and became a strong driving force in effecting the assimilation of the curriculum. Our assessments were closer to what we wanted to accomplish, and the concepts also broke new ground in stating more explicitly what was implicitly expected of students solving problems on tests and in life.

The next step was for the scope and sequence to become a critical supplement to the teacher's guide for the text as the major day-to-day instructional decision determinant—and eventually, as our knowledge and creativity grew, to replace the guide entirely. We also needed to publicize our content document and assessment results, especially to parents.

## Publishing Documents and Sharing Results

Beginning trepidations on the part of parents were first assuaged by informational letters and meetings that described our new curriculum and connected it to national standards and needs. Parents were also encouraged to provide their children with the informal experiences that a modern society does not naturally offer and that many busy parents forget or don't know how to offer. We urged them to build confidence in their offspring, to avoid stereotyping statements such as "boys are better at math" and "I was never good at math," and to refrain from pushing the rote procedures we feared would disrupt the aim of concept development.

The greatest concern was expressed by a small group of parents whose children were traditionally successful at learning the rote procedures. These competitive parents were accustomed to seeing pages of corrected arithmetic algorithms their children had diligently completed. The new conceptual understandings and problem-solving abilities developed by interactive discourse were not easily demonstrated, unless they asked the appropriate questions. Some parents could not be convinced by the classroom teachers of the significance of the ultimate outcomes we desired and had to be personally called or met with.[6]

Knowledgeable parents soon began to appreciate the change. Some who were also teachers in different school districts even sought information for their own classes. We knew they needed more, however, and offered them a course in our new developmental math. It was an opportunity to publicize and demonstrate our new documents. Surprisingly, so many parents were interested that we had to run two sections, each consisting of 10 hours of class. To capture some of the mostly working mothers and fathers, we provided both day and evening sessions and baby-sitting services. A good number of parents looked at our scope and sequence, listened to the developmental psychology, played with the manipulatives, and were sometimes astounded by what they didn't know and could easily learn.

"You mean we can't write anything to help us answer these questions?" the parents asked anxiously when confronted with a dictated arithmetic test of 20 questions. "No, these are all questions we want our students to be able to do mentally," I responded. Nothing I could have told them would have made the point of the new elementary program clearer—especially as we reviewed the thinking processes that should have made each question a cinch.

Our main concerns were for parental interference with what we were doing and for negative feedback about the lack of drill and practice that might create dysfunctional anxiety for teachers. Uninformed parents, who might teach their children the rote procedures they had learned in school as faster and easier ways to get answers, could have corrupted the teacher's purpose of greater understanding. We had to change their values and expectations, but they also needed new capacity. Therefore, we used the concentrated time with parents not only to explain some of the theory behind our new program but to develop new skills that would enable them to enhance their children's knowledge.

Their anxiety about the lack of computation drill and practice was disabused by their realization of the changing needs of society, reassurance that the children would still learn the basic facts (albeit in a different fashion), and by the prospect that they would use the calculators to solve many more problems and see mathematics in a more exciting, challenging, and motivating way. Their commitment to the new approach was finally clinched by the individual mastery reports that documented each child's progress.

Parent evaluations of the course were positive. Suggestions were mainly requests for more of the same and some concern about proper implementation of the new program by some teachers. In any case, parental anxiety definitely decreased, and perhaps an additional support system was generated. Their stakeholder role had added a new dimension of parent expectations that energized the change process. The reality of modern culture, however, is that parents spend less and less time as informal and formal teachers for their children—abdicating that responsibility to formal schooling, organized sports, and television. Despite the enthusiasm of the group, only about half completed the sessions. And what about the hundreds that didn't care? What a pity! Experience mediates learning and learning is directed by human goals. Parents need to expand those experiences and help develop the goals.

## Accountability, Capacity, and Reculturization

Teachers want to know if they have reached their students (Lortie, 1975), and despite the understandable concerns of teacher organizations, they do evaluate themselves through the accomplishments of their students. They hold themselves privately accountable. Perhaps, in an indirect way, the teachers' initial anxiety about the new tests was another manifestation of the importance of successful student assessment as self-affirmation. This was not going to be a remote disconnected intrusion that could, if adverse, be written off as an inadequate and inappropriate measure of effort expended. This was a self- or colleague-generated instrument that could possibly give an unpleasant message. I saw the teachers' concern as an indication of their dedication and commitment to doing and showing their best—an attribute of most educators that is frequently overlooked (Reyes, 1990).

A source of teachers' frustration, however, is in the mismatch between what they have chosen (or has been prescribed for them) to teach and how their performance is measured. If external prescriptions are not followed up by aligned measures of achievement, the prescriptions are soon abandoned for internally comfortable alternatives. Similarly, teacher-generated productive innovations can be stymied by externally imposed irrelevant assessments.

In the South Vale case, reculturization did not occur until the program assessments began to match the prescribed curriculum and the teachers' capacity to implement the new program reached the assimilation level. The content needed to be translated into their own words. The teachers had to either receive the feedback they needed to reassure them of the results of their efforts or realize that they could no longer be comfortable with their private classroom choices not to change. Greta looked anxiously at the poor results of her students on the first administration of the new tests and on the CAT. By the following year, she had caught up to the others (see Chapter 8 for a discussion of the implementation dip). She cared and just needed time and patience.

Confirmation of reculturization and ownership also came that day when Cheryl, who had often articulated reservations but had conscientiously followed the program, burst into an administrators' meeting to report that her students had estimated answers for "uncovered" algorithms. Excitedly she reported, "My students would never in previous years have even tried to do these problems." Their confidence and ability to meet a new and different challenge in mathematics had given their teacher the rare thrill of self-actualization.

## Connecting Curriculum and School Improvement

Hopkins (1990) has found a correlation between teacher self-actualization and implementation of change. He attached a cause and effect relationship to this—with being at the level of self-actualization a characteristic of those who are open to change. This may be the case, but I believe there is also a feedback mechanism through which teachers who have reached their capacity or competence level (Joyce et al., 1990) of an innovation will also have self-actualized because of it. This self-generating relationship could explain why history of change was a better predictor of readiness for change in my previous study (Chapter 3). It may also explain why the positive self-actualizing effects of teachers' engagement in collaborative decision making render them more open to changes in curriculum and to the acceptance of accountability.

In the medical model of a professional culture, accountability is ascribed to peer review as well (Darling-Hammond, 1988). Should school cultures reach the point at which peer review of the accomplishment of outcomes is the norm, collegial reflection on performance and group actualization, interdependent on teacher self-actualization, may overcome the present state of teachers in isolation, burdened by their perceptions of powerlessness. Consensual documentations of curriculum and assessments in combination with changes in school

# Making It Your Own

governance that give teachers greater opportunities to control their environment are starting points, but the ancillary acceptance of group responsibility for client welfare or educational outcomes will require trust building and risk taking by educators and the larger community. Trust building takes time. Time is the subject of the final chapter ahead. I will include a review of how time finally brought the BLTs to the curriculum cogs of content and strategy.

## Notes

1. Results on the CAT were not significantly different for the first year when compared with previous years, although they were somewhat higher for the concepts part of the test. In subsequent years, student results continued to show overall improvement on both this test and on the district's own test, but we usually saw an implementation dip for new teachers. This was consistent during a 6-year period. In the seventh year, an international test placed South Vale 10 to 15 points ahead of the top countries. See Chapter 8 for further discussion.

2. SCIS was a process-based program developed at the University of California at Berkeley that was later commercialized. I brought SCIS to the South Vale School District in 1974. The program remained effective until the mid-1980s when shifts in leadership neglected to keep its momentum going. The new program was cheaper to run because the materials were loaned to the district by our local shared service agency, and it seemed desirable because it was designed to match the state curriculum.

3. In a study by my colleague Edward Westervelt (1993), 75% of the parents who were on our BLTs expressed a reluctance to get involved in curriculum writing.

4. Little of the new knowledge in cognitive science has been incorporated into school curricula or textbooks. Fuson (1990) argues that the present texts may, in fact, contribute to the failure of students to build multiunit concepts.

5. For example, we used the work of Resnick (1983) on part/part/whole in addition and subtraction and the work of Nesher (1988) on multiplicative functions.

6. The parents of gifted children and the children themselves can be the most resistant to change. Like those I noted in Chapter 1, these parents are concerned about competition for college. Because their own children are successful in the present system, they are reluctant to consider new approaches. The children have learned how to deal with the system that rewards a quick right answer and are uncomfortable with open-ended questions and uncertainty.

# 8

# The Fourth Dimension
*Time*

### About Time and Change

"Gather ye rosebuds while ye may, Old time is still a-flying" (Herrick, 1648/1974, p. 121). In other words, time marches on, and you better use it well while it's still there. But where is it? In a surprising twist, as humans reflect on the universality and timelessness of these poetic lines that caution us concretely about the passage of time, scientists ponder about the obscurity of the beginning and end of time, the relativity of its observance, and, as revealed below, about the impossibility that it is ever enough.

> But the universe seems to keep throwing the cosmologists nasty curves, exposing the woeful limitations of their knowledge about how in the apparently allotted time the cosmos evolved from these beginnings to a present day structure of such manifest inhomogeneity. There does not seem to have been enough time. And where and what is all the invisible mass, the so called dark matter, to account for the gravity needed to pull together such vast galactic agglomerations? (Wilford, 1994, p. C1)[1]

Experience with the process of change has confirmed both of these observations about time. Time has always been a significant but underestimated variable in efforts to improve schools. In most cases, impatience with the certainty of making hay while the sun shone took over without regard to the chaos, uncertainty, and the power of the vast and different forces that needed to be understood and dealt with before order would come.

The actions of change require energy that must come from all who are involved in the process, but they require time as well. More than that, they may be governed by time. It is important to understand the intensity of its influence. On the basis of his experience as an external change agent (evocator) helping to restructure three California elementary schools, Donohue (1993) comes to several conclusions about the impact of time. An introduction to his article sums them up: "To Mr. Donohue's mind, restructuring means the formal rearrangement of the use of time in schools to allow them to create and sustain the kind of interactive culture and supporting infrastructure they need to improve student learning" (p. 298).

A comprehensive report to the secretary of education by the National Education Commission on Time and Learning (1994) considers time an overall and critical limiting factor in school reform. The report identifies schools as "prisoners of time" and calls it their warden. Although it is obvious from previous chapters that I do not believe that time is quite that simply the sole variable of restructuring and reculturization, the many aspects of time are so significant that I have found it useful to organize my conclusions in relationship to this variable.

Time, as a variable in the process of change, may be considered from three perspectives: time as a *resource* to do what is necessary; time as the component of *timetables or the fourth dimension* over which we can plan for, experience, and measure change—or regress to prior states; and time as *timeliness*, or the probability of success for a new state on the basis of the nature of affecting variables at the particular moment—serendipity.

## Time as a Resource for Collaboration

Donohue (1993) found, as did we in South Vale, that the lack of sufficient time for teachers to work together was a great source of stress. Although he could buy the time for teachers, they didn't have the space to install it. The National Education Commission on Time and Learning (1994) offers several recommendations to overcome this, but all involve extensions to the school calendar because they place great emphasis on the inadequacy of the total time for learning.

In South Vale, more time was needed for teachers to plan collaboratively and share their research. Lack of time produced leadership burnout if burdens were not shared and if the payoff was not visible (Chapter 6). Even Elaine, Lila, and the others, who were mentors for the new teachers, were not compensated by the district for their mentoring time. They settled for the satisfactions of collegiality, group actualization, and college credit. For some teachers, it was more important to use the scheduled time of a "free period" to check student work than to use it to learn from colleagues or plan with them for long-term school improvement.

We were more successful with shared reflections and other capacity-building activities related to the changes in math when we were able to buy time for teachers with substitutes. But teachers still had anxiety about the loss of contact time with students. The National Education Commission on Time and Learning (1994) report notes that new teaching strategies can require 50 hours of instruction, practice, and teaching and 50 days of external technical assistance. That was not nearly enough for our changes in mathematics!

Sandy's stress and Greta's refusal to take in-service courses or observe models and the reluctance of many teachers to become involved in SBCDM are readily attributable to the conflict that arises when teachers have to make choices between time in the classroom and time to learn new methods or make collegial decisions. Teachers should not have to make these choices! Time for professional growth and responsibilities needs to be part of the educational culture, as it is in countries such as Japan (Stevenson, 1987, 1988). The National Education Commission on Time and Learning (1994) suggests that it is not "a frill or add on, but . . . a major aspect of the agreement between teachers and districts" (p. 36).

Donohue and the commission suggest that the only way to achieve this is to completely restructure the school day and year to build in time for collegial enterprise. I agree with them but fear that the cost and departure from the tradition of many stakeholders will be great hurdles to overcome. Meanwhile, viable alternatives may exist. The University of the State of New York (1990) suggests a number of ways that time for collaborative planning can be built into the day and year. Some of its many ideas are listed below (in italics) along with my suggestions:

1. *Investing time initially to organize procedures and responsibilities for collaborative planning.* This will be helpful, but even more important is knowing the decision-making paths and terminals beforehand. It will not only save time but also prevent frustration and clarify the sources of power (and perhaps indicate how they may need to be changed).

2. *Building time for collaborative planning into the master schedule.* Shared planning periods are an example of this. The National Education Commission on Time and Learning (1994) also suggests adding days to the school year, lengthening the day, and rotating teachers through the year.

3. *Considering long-term student assignments to teams of teachers and/or employing cluster groups of teachers as an alternative to "one teacher, one group" organization.* I have seen both of these suggestions successfully implemented (Solomon, 1994). Team teaching also breaks away from the solitude of the traditional model and provides the opportunity for reflective interactions. An extra teacher on a team assures the continuity of instruction. While one or two team members participate in schoolwide governance, curriculum contract and assessment development, or the sharing of new ideas through modeling, students can deal with familiar and knowing adults.

4. *Budgeting for additional paid preparation time, days for collaborative planning, and extra personnel including regular teachers, substitutes, and teaching assistants.* There are limits to stretching teachers' time and energy. To avoid burnout, the stress of added burdens for schoolwide consensus building and decision making must be recognized. For example, in South Vale, Sandy should have had someone to do her BLT typing and her lunch duty.

5. *Reviewing contractual restrictions that hinder opportunities for joint planning.* Everyone needs to work together on this. Every source of power may have to give some to gain more.

This last suggestion can be related to another consideration that may be the possible solution to burnout problems. The teachers in South Vale had no obligation to participate in SBCDM. *Participation in school decision making must be a cultural obligation, not a voluntary gift of time.* As Sarason (1993) suggests, the training of teachers and administrators should include preparation for this. If everyone in South Vale had participated in the process of SBCDM, the energy drain would have been less, the commitment would have been greater, and burnout may not have occurred.

Although Donohue (1993) suggests that schools are small enough to have direct democracy rather than representative democracy—and I know that teachers have not yet learned to trust each other—I think that if everyone is involved in some way, teachers can learn to accept decisions on which they have not individually voted, especially in areas in which they have not had traditional autonomy. I do not think educators have the capacity, the time, or the energy for direct democracy when decisions are broader and affect many. We need to know more about consensus building and the mechanisms of what Donohue calls "shared influence" (p. 299). But everyone's voice should be listened to, and everyone should be doing something that goes beyond the individual classroom. The workload must be shared!

Everyone does not have be involved in the same cluster or at the same time. Collegial cultures can be protean with many sources of leadership and with different clusters of colleagues concentrating on different needs.[2] From McNeil and McNeil's (1994) perspective, "limiting the function of the school based SDM (shared decision making) committee will probably render them more powerful than an SDM committee with a wider range of responsibilities" (p. 259). The South Vale math needs assessment committee and follow-up planning groups are examples of clusters concentrating on curriculum while other groups (the BLTs) focused on other schoolwide organizational decisions. The standards teams that are presently working at developing district standards in South Vale and in many parts of the country, one set at a time, are other examples. Their efforts on the specifics can be separately conducted, but these collegial efforts need to be interactive and integrated with each other and designed to achieve congruence of voices and vision on the more general and overlapping missions.

Clusters of teachers working on curriculum, assessment, or organization can function at a variety of levels: two or three peers at a grade level, school-based clusters across grade levels, interschool clusters to search for continuity of local standards, and clusters within a state and across states in professional groups to agree on the common standards for broader outcomes and frameworks. Teacher-leaders and administrators from different school districts can work together to share leadership strategies and problem solutions.

The voices of parents also need to be heard. Parents can be of great help (see Chapter 7), but they need capacity building, and time is a resource for them also. In today's society in which everyone works, they may have only limited time for involvement. Jean Brown, a parent and BLT member mentioned in Chapter 3, expressed it with the following anecdote:

> There are numerous households with dual working people, and they would like to participate. But, the time constraints are awfully hard sometimes. Fortunately the meetings are on Wednesdays and Fridays. . . . I don't work on those days. . . . Night would be hard. I have three children, and there is homework and household responsibilities. It puts a certain amount of strain on you. . . . I was looking over the homework guidelines about making time to talk to your kids and I was laughing because the last time my husband came home early from work we took the kids to the park . . . and by the time we came back, we worked like maniacs to finish the homework. . . . At least we had some time together, but that had to be scheduled too. (Westervelt, 1993, p. 140)

The solutions to this problem of limited resources of time for parents are as varied as those for the teacher time problem. To begin with, parents should be offered some selectivity. They do not have to be involved in every committee function—they may not be interested in some of the tasks. Baby-sitting by high school students, rotating teams of parents, and weekend meetings might be useful—and how about a no-homework night when parents need to come to school? In the future, extended days or years for students may be bartered in exchange for parent involvement.

## Time as a Resource for Instruction

The National Education Commission on Time and Learning (1994) sees a shortage of time for instruction as a major issue for schools in the United States. The commission views the fixed clocks and calendars of schools as a "major design flaw" and a barrier to their ability to respond to "the great changes that have reshaped life outside the school" (p. 13). The report compares the academic time—time spent on actual instruction as opposed to other school activities—in this country with that of other developed countries and notes the great deficiency (Japan, France, and Germany all have more than double the academic time in the final 4 years). The commission closely links additional instructional time to any hope for meeting the goals of higher standards.

Time was an issue in South Vale when we strived for the higher standard of mathematical understanding and concept development. It required the cumbersome use of manipulatives, and we asked teachers to abandon the traditional worksheets that they often used to control how they used their time. "There isn't enough time for it all," the teachers complained. They could not, at first, envision the ability of the new method to accomplish their goals and felt that they had to continue old methods as well. Time is always a real constraint. But if teachers accommodate for change by trying to fit in the new with the old, it is further constrictive. And if, as suggested by Sizer, "less is more" (quoted in Brandt, 1988, p. 32) and vast unconnected or uncategorized bits of information are short-lived in memory (Anderson, 1990), it is a dysfunctional and poorly grounded solution. We found more efficient ways to use the time: Time for concept building could easily be gained from the abandonment of obsolete drill and practice on complex algorithms that a calculator was better at solving. Schools must make some of the critical curriculum choices that I suggested in the previous chapter, and present comforts of practice may need to be abandoned.

This is not easy for educators. On one occasion, a teacher who complained about the lack of time for the new mathematics goals invited me to see her class perform a series of intricate dances that one of her parents had taught the children during the school day. It was obvious that learning the dances had taken much instructional time, but the teacher was proud of this activity and the children and parents were too. Given the time limitations, one dance and a connection of the rhythm of the dance to mathematics would have been sufficient—but old habits and reward systems are difficult to abandon.

Educators need to rethink the way we allocate our time and organize the fragments of our curriculum into it. Another solution suggested in the University of the State of New York (1990) document on managing time is to connect overlapping content areas via interdisciplinary activities. The streamlining of curriculum in this and other ways is even suggested by the usually content-minded American

Association for the Advancement of Science (1989): "To ensure the scientific literacy of all students, curricula must be changed to reduce the sheer amount of material covered; to weaken or eliminate rigid subject matter boundaries; to pay more attention to the connections among science, mathematics and technology" (p. 5).

## Time for Passage: The Implementation Dip

As we hurtle through time, things happen to delay and accelerate us, but no matter how fast and erratically we move, there is always a minimum interval from start to finish. As schools implement change, time is needed for administrators, teachers, parents, and students to gain their new capacity and grow comfortable with their new methods and with a new culture. Developmental time for teachers and students needs to be accounted for in our expectations. At first, the South Vale third-grade students were somewhat hampered by previously learned rote procedures; in contrast, the younger students were immediately successful. In time, those who had grown up with the new approach were even more successful because they had developed the habits of mind that increased their ability to construct new and complex concepts.

Analyses of test results indicated that the level of teachers' involvement in professional development and experience time with the math program was responsible for some of the variance in students' performance. Building everyone's capacity is not an overnight task (Chapters 6 and 7). Each time a new group of teachers was added, a statistically significant difference in the achievement of their students was measured on both the CAT and the district's tests when compared with the students of their more experienced colleagues.[3]

The exception to this was the first-year pilot group, whose students never lost ground on the CAT. Perhaps the intensive commitment of the teachers and close support overcame the problems of change, and they quickly became comfortable. It may have also been the Hawthorne effect, in which improvement occurs at first just because of the newness. In most cases, however, schools engaged in change, especially if they are using old assessments, must prepare for the implementation dip (Fullan, 1994), a decline in measured outcomes until capacity is sufficient.

The Hawthorne effect may have also been operational in the first year of change at the high school, in which we had eliminated

# The Fourth Dimension: Time

tracking and placed almost all of the ninth-grade students in Regents classes (Chapter 5). Initial feedback was encouraging. The students were motivated by the higher expectations, and teachers felt that they had a chance for success. In any case, the attitude of the students was much better than it had been in non-Regents classes; at midyear, the two teachers were reluctant to give up on anyone. As I went over the class lists with Deanna and George, they kept saying, "I think they can do it!"

Regents exam results confirmed their expectations. About 55% of the special students, who never would have been in Regents-level classes, passed the Regents exam; most of those who failed the exam passed the course for local credit. In addition, teachers of other Regents-level classes were similarly successful. A skeptical staff member hypothesized that the reason why so many passed the Regents exam was that some of these special students had taken pre-algebra the previous year. Analyses revealed that the 9th graders in the group passed at a higher rate than the 10th graders who had had the pre-algebra!

Most of the high school staff were still convinced, however, that it would be better if these students had a longer time to complete the curriculum. But as I have previously noted, the power of the schedule overruled, discouraged the staff, and may have influenced their spirit. Less successful results occurred with the special Regents group the following year—even Deanna was disappointed. It was a delayed implementation dip—but we stuck to our goal for equity.

The extension of time for these students was finally allowed for the 1991-1992 school year, but by then the school culture had changed. The high school BLT's goal of higher expectations and the math teachers' belief in it has had a definite lasting effect on the cultural values of students. They signed up for Regents math classes at unprecedented levels, with enrollment in these classes moving from an overall average of 52% of the total number of students through the junior year in 1986-1987 to 76% of the total enrollment in 1990-1991. Out of the entire ninth grade, only one small group of students were recommended for the special support of the three-semester Regents-level class. Similar increases in Regents enrollments have also occurred in other subject areas.

With the exception of the middle school, which plunged quickly into curriculum, the BLTs were busy at first with the school climate factors—a type of implementation dip, if one is looking at product

**TABLE 8.1** Excerpts From the Park Lane Building Plan 1990-1991

| Area and Activity Description | Person Responsible | Persons Involved | Timeline | Attainment Measures |
|---|---|---|---|---|
| Inviting School Atmosphere: To analyze targeted areas, as identified by our survey in terms of the inviting school philosophy | Teacher and principal | BLT and staff | December 1990 | Analysis completed |
| Planning for Academic Excellence: To provide dialogue time for teachers to communicate expectations regarding a variety of curriculum issues and classroom activity | 2 teachers | All teachers | All faculty meetings | Provided |
| To provide teachers the opportunity to visit one another's classrooms | Principal | Interested teachers | Continuous school year | Visits facilitated |
| To decide on the use of cultural arts funds to enhance integrated curriculum | Director and teacher | 5 teachers | January 1991 | Funds allocated |
| To set periodic meetings with support teachers and classroom teachers to analyze scores and monitor progress | Principal | Teachers | Continuous | Meetings held |

solely in terms of student achievement. But by the third year, they became involved in several curriculum and assessment functions. The yearly plan for the Park Lane BLT included several of these. Table 8.1 is an excerpt from their plan for that year, which shows concentration on some important student-centered items.

## Timetables and Leadership Energy

Notice the timetable in Table 8.1 and how teacher-leaders were beginning to have some control and accept some responsibility for getting things done. Sarason (1972) says that leaders of new settings have timetables that create pressure to get started and "a present

# The Fourth Dimension: Time

dominated and tyrannized by a future which when it arrives is not the one imagined" (p. 63). The pressure of timetables that are created by internal forces (such as teachers' and leaders' own imperatives) and external forces (such as standardized tests) affect the delicate balance of human comfort with present practice and the motivation to change.

In a more recent retrospective on changes in school governance, Sarason (1993) writes that when teachers in their new roles were asked to accept the responsibility for effecting change, their actions "collided with the need for and difficulty of unlearning old ways," and they "underestimated what one confronts in sustaining a change" (p. 20). Change requires the passage of adequate amounts of time; teachers and principals need to practice their new methods and feel the rewards of new practice before they can comfortably abandon the old. Leadership support from the evocator of change is needed to make that passage through time a smooth one.

Although the ultimate future in regard to the South Vale mathematics program change was not too different from my vision, the timetable and process of reaching it were. The need for new capacity was more than I had envisioned, as was the resistance encountered. As I reported in Chapters 5 and 6, leadership energy in the form of support was needed to balance the pressure of timetables and the struggle for power and control in a productive way.

The graph in Figure 8.1 is an example of the fluctuations through a timetable (albeit an after-the-fact one) of the varying levels of energy required for leadership pressure and support and the building of new capacity for teachers through peer and self-reflections. It represents my perception of the changing needs during a 6-year period of five phases of the elementary mathematics change: preparation, trial, systemic adoption, maintenance and refinement, and review and revision (minor and major revisions may be needed at any stage, however).

## Controlling Timetables

Close engagement with a system often prevents people from seeing it in its entirety. Because seeing a system as a whole is a useful tack, from time to time we need to take a step back from our own absorbing piece to see how it all fits together. It is also helpful to break

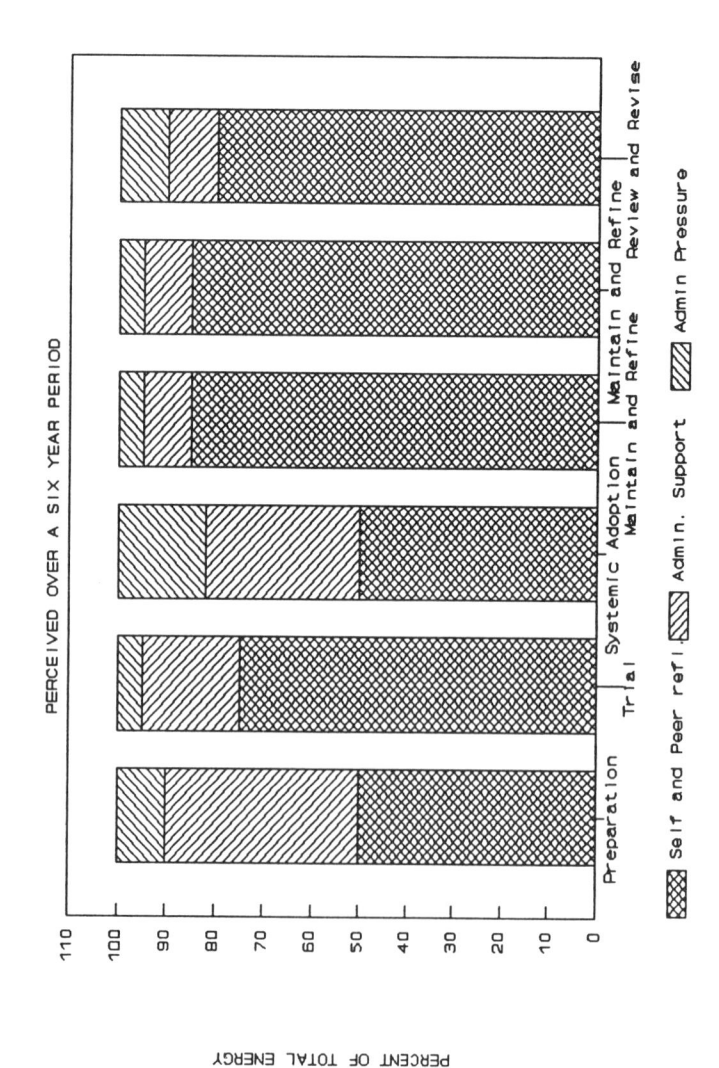

**Figure 8.1.** Energy Expenditures for Change

# The Fourth Dimension: Time

away completely to look at other systems to strengthen the holistic picture with analogies. I had the unique opportunity to sit in on a debriefing meeting for team leaders in the research and development division of an international high-tech firm, at which my daughter, Nancy, is a new manager (it was mother-daughter day).

"I like your style, Nancy," I told her later, "you listened most of the time." "I'm an enabler," she replied, "and many of the people I enable know more than I do—as a matter of fact, they may also earn more than I do. It is my responsibility to keep the pieces working smoothly and together, and my responsibility to see that the resources and rewards for success or grief for failure are equitably distributed."

Nancy had discovered that giving power (see Chapter 4) was an effective form of leading professionals. She extended this to giving power over timetables, the topic of their discussion. As so frequently happens in school systems, other people's timetables were creating pressure on those who had to meet them. I heard the following suggestion:

> It is best to present your group with a suggested timetable and ask them to react to its feasibility in terms of their own needs and capability. People will respond in different ways: They will suggest minor corrections, or they will accept your timetable and try to meet it, or they will not respond at all and go on their merry way. They will all, however, take some ownership, and what you then have to do is monitor their progress and help them when necessary.

I liked this method and realized that timetables are not usually presented to others that way. Often they are set by leaders with insufficient input from those who must meet them. The result is resistance. Far worse are the instances when control of timetables is at first left completely to the individuals who must meet them, and then the leader decides that he or she cannot live with those choices.

South Vale's change to SBCDM had little leadership support and no coherence in vision from central office for the principals and teachers who were engaged in a time- and energy-consuming process. But in their planning, the principals and teachers had opportunities for peer reflection and some control of timetables. Despite the missing leadership needed to get started, their own capacity to lead grew—at least until they burned out because the total time and energy resource was insufficient and the power struggle debilitating.

Reflection on the timetables for curriculum and governance changes, however, reveals that both of them were presented in a less-than-productive manner. The timetable for curriculum change was too hurried and had insufficient input from the BLTs when it shifted from volunteers to a mandate. The timetable for the management changes had little direction beforehand, and limits and dead ends became clear only after the fact. Teachers need more control over their timetables, but the limits of the timetables need to be clear, and teachers need to be held accountable for them.

## Expecting and Preventing Regression

There is much current interest in the theory of chaos, which although it has mythological origins as well, is based on the ideas of entropy. Essentially these ideas hypothesize or philosophize about the constant reciprocal relationship between order and disorder. Evidence shows that the order of the universe arises from the disorder and that a force pushes for order, but at the same time, an opposing force pushes for disorder. The passage of time can help bring about change; time can also destroy it.

Another of Donohue's (1993) insights—one that I have alluded to previously—is that schools need capable principals who can help teacher-leaders become strong enough to take over their responsibilities. If one of the problems for schools is their inconsistent leadership by transient principals and central office administrators who are career bound and mobile, the solution is to have teacher-leaders with more consistency of vision for them and their teams. For a while, I thought that the Park Lane BLT, whose yearly plan excerpts appear in Table 8.1, might be heading in that direction.

Perhaps, in reflecting on their previous unhappy situation with their principal, Anne (see Chapter 4), they adopted the motto "Together We Can"; the best summary of what happened at Park Lane for the next few years would be "Together We Did." They were the first to move from the general climate elements to concerns about monitoring their progress and defining their curriculum, often inviting the directors to their planning meetings and working with them as smaller clusters on specific curriculum projects. Instead of the directors setting the pace, a request for written outcomes came from the Park Lane BLT. At meetings they looked at the socioeconomically disaggregated test results and planned strategies to overcome any differences between the groups—including interclass observations by teachers. The experienced teachers continued their own efforts with the new direction for mathematics and led the newcomers. I am confident that the changes will be maintained.

Park Lane was selected for presidential recognition as an outstanding "Blue Ribbon" school and designated as an "Inviting School" by the Alliance for Invitational Education. They also quickly shifted from the effective schools needs assessment and criteria to their own more open-ended assessments. Anne consulted her BLT on almost every important school decision, and the team played a critical role in choosing new staff and in changing schedules. The teachers used their power to modify Anne's priorities. For example, they successfully protested her encouragement of timed-facts competitions, which were not congruent with the mathematics program goals. Although they still relied on Anne for many of the routine management tasks, there was a general feeling that they had much more control—at least within the fiscal and personnel constraints imposed by the central office.

And then, as time passed, three things happened: A new superintendent came, many teachers retired and were replaced by new young people, and those who remained burned out and left the BLTs. The new superintendent was strong, but his vision did not include sharing power with building teams. There was no gain of power at first and then some diminution. In response, Alan and others left from the critical leadership of the DLT. As Nate told us (see Chapter 1), "The building teams don't do very much anymore."

The new superintendent recognized the potential of the existing culture, however, and used it to accomplish his vision of advertising the success of the many fine things that had happened in South Vale. He was successful at this because his incentives for teachers to take early retirement resulted in replacing the strong but burned out BLTs with teams that consisted mostly of the new young untenured teachers. They were struggling to succeed in their classrooms but joined the teams and worked hard to demonstrate their commitment to the culture and to their building principal.

They were, however, too insecure and not really interested in control or power over what was happening to them or to their nonparticipating colleagues, and they had little capacity to assume power. Soon they were resented by the experienced teachers who felt that the new team members were making uninformed decisions that did not listen to their voices. "They don't know what is going on. Anne sets the agenda and they just do what she says," one of the original Park Lane team members complained to me. "Be patient," I consoled her (after admonishing her for not taking a more active role herself). Teacher leadership within the teams was recycled in a different form, and a new implementation dip occurred—but the new team members were being acculturated to an important concept, and soon they would gain the necessary capacity.

The superintendent, anxious to cut administrative expenses, also consolidated the roles of the two curriculum directors. One person is now in charge of all K-12 subjects. Fortunately, the elementary math changes were so ingrained in the teachers' culture that teacher-leadership took over. Several of the experienced staff, including Elaine and Lila, became teacher mentors for the newcomers. As a consultant from my new position, I was able to offer some support for this effort. But there still was the usual implementation dip, and, as Elaine's lament revealed, a lack of sufficient help. "I'm too busy helping everyone," she complained. "Not only are the new teachers asking for assistance but last year's teachers as well."

Although a recently administered international math test has demonstrated that South Vale is still successful, I know that the effort to maintain quality in mathematics and in other subjects as well will require leadership attention to returning order from the disorder that the forces of chaos are bound to conjure. But the serendipity of timing has strengthened my hope for an emerging renewal of this leadership from the inchoate new culture of teacher-leaders.

## The Serendipity of Timing

No doubt the universe is controlled by natural laws, but those laws are based on humanly observed present states. This subjects the laws, themselves, to humans' own limitations and makes them easily mutable by unforeseen events. In addition, the laws recognize that present states can be interrupted or promoted by predictable forces of known or unknown probability, and probability is related to chance. A single comet at the right place and time destroyed millions of years of success for the dinosaurs. Unhappy chance can encumber or kind serendipity can assure the success of the process of any school change.

## The Fourth Dimension: Time

Tyack and Tobin (1994) examine the history of school change and compare successes and failures. One of their conclusions is that "the timing of reforms in the institutional life cycle is important" (p. 476). There was kind serendipity for me when the highly acclaimed NCTM standards (1989b) were published a year after South Vale began the mathematics changes, and serendipity, I hope, will also play a role in continuing the reculturization in the district. The New York State Education Department has mandated both the restructuring of schools toward SBCDM and the development of new local standards. Propitiously, a new group of BLT teacher-leaders is growing up and gaining capacity in the appropriate culture. Other clusters are already getting practice in setting their standards and developing authentic assessments. If they look at their history with care, they have the elementary mathematics model to follow.

The evocator of change cannot always count on serendipity and must expect that the "best-laid schemes o' mice and men gang aft a-gley" (Burns, 1785/1974, p. 25). Meanwhile, it is best to operate with knowledge of the observable natural laws, some of which I have shared from my perspective in this book. Sharing research observations, listening to voices, and connecting to history make a good beginning; concurrently, each of us engaged in the process of educating others must become more reflective and less bounded in time and place. And then we must get going: We will never be able to adjust to rapidly changing societal needs until we do.

Fullan (1994) has suggested that the way change should happen compares to a metaphor of *ready, fire, aim*. He feels that K-12 schools have started with *fire* before they are ready, universities have spent too much time on *ready*, and state education departments are hung up on *aiming*. I have also heard others suggest that outcomes and final direction or vision may not be clear until after getting started. I agree but prefer a glimpse of the target and the ability to alter the course of my arrow as the wind changes. Modern weaponry already has that capability.

Although SBCDM may be among the educational reforms that will help make the nation's schools more responsive to changing needs, this reform and others can expect to encounter an opposing wave of history and tradition; an ineluctable lack of time and, perhaps, serendipity; and a hesitation to share trust, power, responsibility, and resources. Educators may need to make some adjustments in plans for changes in school governance as we proceed, and we should consider concurrent efforts in program reform to reach the common goal of improved education. That doesn't mean that we shouldn't try school governance reform; I just wouldn't put all of my eggs in one basket.

After a 7-year trial in South Vale, a spark of optimism still exists in the willingness of almost everyone to continue, in the progress that has been made in the reculturization of school climates, and in the realization that differently structured collegial decision-making groups can effectively coexist but may be at their best when integrated with each other. Optimism also lies in the hope that the history of the successes—and serendipity—will outweigh the failures and overcome the latest implementation dip.

## Looking Ahead in Time

As I contemplate the future from the vantage of the present, it is done with retrospect, particularly in reference to the variables that shaped the nature and influenced the progress of the many program changes and the more recent cultural change in which I was a player. My training in biology offers another perspective. Evolution on this earth has proceeded generally on a course from the simple to the complex, but a number of backward steps occurred on the way. The general direction for humans has been an increase in cognitive ability that has given us greater control over the environment, although that control has not always been good for it and may, in many cases, have interfered with natural evolutionary processes. Humans may even have to take some backward steps.

For schools, as the process of education becomes ever more complicated in its response to the rapidly growing complexity of humanly created environments and the probability of unforeseen events beyond human abilities to predict, we need evocator-leaders at every step. We need leaders with visions from many sources: teachers, administrators, and others who can help map and remap the future courses with respect for the history and voices that frame them, who help each person gain new capacity, and who are willing to share their power to garner the energies of many and achieve greater effect. We need leaders who consider carefully the limits of time as a resource and as the fourth dimension through which we travel. And from my perspective, having seen so many things pass

# The Fourth Dimension: Time

quickly by, the rate at which we move through time has accelerated. These limits may require some backward steps and hard choices, because we can neither do it all nor control it all. Good leaders, however, can help us pass successfully through what may perhaps in the future be perceived only as the history of an evolutionary or slowly changing step in time.

Thoreau (1849/1893, p. 226) opined with poetic optimism about the passage of time:

> Then idle time ran gadding by
> And left me with eternity alone.
> I hear beyond the range of sound,
> I see beyond the verge of sight.

But do I?

## Notes

1. This excerpt is from "Big Bangs Defenders Weigh Fudge Factor, a Blunder of Einstein's, as Fix for New Crisis," by J. N. Wilford, November 1, 1994, *New York Times*, p. C1. Copyright © 1994 by The New York Times Company. Reprinted by permission.

2. My colleague John DiNatale (1990) discovered that leadership in South Vale was protean, but our collegial clusters were also protean.

3. Our analyses explored the relationship between the individual teacher's level of training and implementation experience with the new math program (the independent variable) and the performance of the teacher's class on the administered tests (the dependent variable). The computed chi-square value of 9.1 and $r$ value of .615 were significant at the .005 level and indicated only that the classes of teachers who had more preparation and experience did better on the two performance measures than would be expected if the teacher's preparation was not a variable affecting the students' performance.

# Epilogue

The most current research by neuroscientists on how the human brain functions has identified timing as a significant element in the ability to consciously perceive (Blakeslee, 1995). Apparently, the brain does not take in whole images. Instead, it consolidates fragments of information from the senses and from various parts of the brain to form whole images. This fusion does not seem to occur in a place (like a screen); instead, it occurs as a synchronization in time. The brain fires these fragments so that they come together at one time. Scientists are now in search of the signals or traffic lights that can control this timing.

One can conclude from this that disorders of perception could very well be caused by dysfunctional timing. Perhaps our difficulties with the process of school change are similarly caused by dysfunctions in timing. Good leaders can be our traffic lights, but they need to know about the fragments of their cultures and be careful about time.

# References

Anderson, J. R. (1990). *The adaptive character of thought.* Hillsdale, NJ: Lawrence Erlbaum.
American Association for the Advancement of Science. (1989). *2061: Science for all Americans.* Washington, DC: Author.
Argyris, C. (1976). *Increasing leadership effectiveness.* New York: John Wiley.
Baroody, A. J. (1987). *Children's mathematical thinking.* New York: Teachers College Press.
Barr, R. (1988). Conditions influencing content taught in nine fourth grade mathematics classrooms. *The Elementary School Journal, 88,* 388-410.
Barth, R. (1988). School: A community of leaders. In A. Lieberman (Ed.), *Building a professional culture in schools* (pp. 129-147). New York: Teachers College Press.
Bennis, W., & Nanus, B. (1985). *Leaders: The strategies for taking charge.* New York: Harper & Row.
Berger, R. (1991, March 9). Miami finds mixed results in Fernandez's school plan. *New York Times,* p. 25.
Blakeslee, S. (1995, March 21). How the brain might work: A new theory of consciousness. *New York Times,* pp. C1, C10.
Brandt, R. (1988). On changing secondary schools: A conversation with Ted Sizer. *Educational Leadership, 45*(5), 30-34.
Burns, R. (1974). To a mouse. In M. H. Abrams, E. T. Donaldson, H. Smith, R. M. Adams, S. H. Monk, L. Lipsky, G. H. Ford, & D. Daiches (Eds.), *Norton anthology of English literature* (Vol. 2, p. 25). New York: Norton. (Original work published 1785)
Carnegie Commision on Science, Technology and Government. (1991). *In the national interest: The federal government in the reform of K-12 math and science education.* New York: Author.
Carpenter, T. P., Fennema, E., Peterson, P., & Carey, D. (1988). Teachers' pedagogical content knowledge of students' problem solving in elementary arithmetic. *Journal for Research in Mathematics Education, 19*(5), 385-401.

Cobb, P. (1990). Multiple perspectives. In L. P. Steffe & T. Wood (Eds.), *Transforming children's mathematics education: International perspectives* (pp. 200-215). Hillsdale, NJ: Lawrence Erlbaum.

Cogan, M. (1973). *Clinical supervision*. Boston: Houghton Mifflin.

Cooper, M. (1988). Whose culture is it, anyway? In A. Lieberman (Ed.), *Building a professional culture in schools* (pp. 129-147). New York: Teachers College Press.

Cox, P. (1983). Complementary roles in successful change. *Educational Leadership, 41*(3), 10-13.

Crandall, D. P. (1983). The teacher's role in school improvement. *Educational Leadership, 41*(3), 6-9.

Darling-Hammond, L. (1988). Policy and professionalism. In A. Lieberman (Ed.), *Building a professional culture in schools* (pp. 55-77). New York: Teachers College Press.

Darling-Hammond, L. (1990). Instructional policy into practice: The power of the bottom over the top. *Educational Evaluation and Policy Analysis, 12*(3), 233-241.

Deal, T. E. (1990). Reframing reform. *Educational Leadership, 47*(8), 612.

DiNatale, J. (1990). *The protean nature of instructional leadership: A study in the relationship between the central office curriculum director and principal*. Unpublished doctoral dissertation, Fordham University, New York.

Donohue, T. (1993). Finding the way: Structure, time and culture in school improvement. *Phi Delta Kappan, 74*, 298-305.

Dossey, J. A., Mullis, I. V. S., Lindquist, M. M., & Chambers, D. L. (1988). *The mathematics report card: Are we measuring up?* Princeton, NJ: Educational Testing Service.

Edmonds, R. R. (1983). Programs of school improvement: An overview. *Educational Leadership, 40*(4), 4-11.

English, F. W., & Steffy, B. E. (1982). Curriculum as a strategic management tool. *Educational Leadership, 39*(8), 276-278.

Finn, C. E., Jr. (1990). The biggest reform of all. *Phi Delta Kappan, 71*, 585-592.

Firestone, W. A., & Pennell, J. R. (1993). Teacher commitment, working conditions, and differential incentive policies. *Review of Educational Research, 63*(4), 489-525.

French, W. L., & Bell, C. H. (1973). *Organization development*. Englewood Cliffs, NJ: Prentice Hall.

Fullan, M. (1982). *The meaning of educational change*. New York: Teachers College Press.

Fullan, M. (1990). Staff development, innovation, and institutional development. In B. Joyce (Ed.), *Changing school cultures through staff development* (pp. 3-25). Alexandria, VA: Association for Supervision and Curriculum Development.

Fullan, M. (1994, October 28). *Managing change*. Suffern: New York State Association for Supervision and Curriculum Development.

Fullan, M., Bennett, B., & Bennett, C. R. (1990). Linking classroom and school improvement. *Educational Leadership, 47*(8), 13-19.

Fuson, K. C. (1990). Issues in place-value and multidigit addition and subtraction learning and teaching. *Journal of Research in Mathematics Education, 21*, 273-280.

Gay, J., & Cole, M. (1967). *The new mathematics and old culture*. New York: Holt, Rinehart & Winston.

Ginsburg, H. P., Posner, J., & Russell, R. (1981). The development of knowledge concerning written arithmetic. *International Journal of Psychology, 16*, 13-34.

Glasser, W. (1986). *Control theory in the classroom*. New York: Harper & Row.

Glatthorn, A. A. (1987). *Curriculum renewal*. Alexandria, VA: Association for Supervision and Curriculum Development.

Goodson, I. F. (1992). Sponsoring the teachers voice: Teachers' lives and teacher development. In A. Hargreaves & M. Fullan (Eds.), *Understanding teacher development* (pp. 110-121). London: Cassell.

# References

Hansen, K. H. (1967). Planning for changes in education. In E. Morphet & C. Ryan (Eds.), *Designing education for the future* (pp. 24-25). New York: Citation.

Herrick, R. (1974). The Hesperides: To the virgins, to make much of time. In H. Maclean (Ed.), *Ben Johnson and the cavalier poets* (p. 121). New York: Norton. (Original work published 1648)

Hopkins, D. (1990). Integrating staff development and school improvement: A study of teacher personality and school climate. In B. Joyce (Ed.), *Changing school culture through staff development* (pp. 41-67). Alexandria, VA: Association for Supervision and Curriculum Development.

Huberman, M. (1992). Teacher development and instructional mastery. In A. Hargeaves & M. Fullan (Eds.), *Understanding teacher development* (pp. 122-142). London: Cassell.

Huberman, M., & Miles, M. (1984). *Innovation up close*. New York: Plenum.

Huberman, M., & Miles, M. (1986). Rethinking the quest for school improvement: Some findings from the DESSI study. In A. Lieberman (Ed.), *Rethinking school improvement* (pp. 61-81). New York: Teachers College Press.

Johnson, D. W., & Johnson, R. T. (1989). *Cooperation and competition: Theory and research*. Edina, MN: Interaction.

Johnson, R. T., Johnson, D. W., & Johnson-Holubec, E. (1987). *Revised circles of learning: Cooperation in the classroom*. Edina, MN: Interaction.

Joyce, B., Bennett, B., & Bennett, C. R. (1990). The self educating teacher: Empowering teachers through research. In B. Joyce (Ed.), *Changing school cultures through staff development* (pp. 26-40). Alexandria, VA: Association for Supervision and Curriculum Development.

Joyce, B. R., & Showers, B. (1980). Improving inservice training: The messages of research. *Educational Leadership, 37*(5), 379-385.

Kerman, S. (1979). Teacher expectations and student achievement. *Phi Delta Kappan, 60*, 716-718.

Kilpatrick, J. (1985). *Academic preparation in mathematics*. New York: The College Board.

Lave, J. (1977). Cognitive consequences of traditional apprenticeship training in West Africa. *Anthropology and Education Quarterly, 8*, 177-180.

Lieberman, A., & Miller, L. (1986). School improvement: Themes and variations. In A. Lieberman (Ed.), *Rethinking school improvement* (pp. 96-111). New York: Teachers College Press.

Lieberman, A., & Miller, L. (1990). Restructuring schools: What matters and what works. *Phi Delta Kappan, 71*, 759-764.

Lieberman, A., Saxl, E. R., & Miles, M. (1988). Teacher leadership: Ideology and practice. In A. Lieberman (Ed.), *Building a professional culture in schools* (pp. 148-166). New York: Teachers College Press.

Little, J. W. (1988). Assessing the prospects for teacher leadership. In A. Lieberman (Ed.), *Building a professional culture in schools* (pp. 78-106). New York: Teachers College Press.

Little, J. W. (1992). Teachers' professional development in a climate of educational reform. *Educational Evaluation and Policy Analysis, 15*(2), 129-151.

Longstreet, W. S., & Shane, H. G. (1993). *Curriculum for a new millennium*. Needham, MA: Allyn & Bacon.

Lortie, D. C. (1975). *School teacher*. Chicago: University of Chicago Press.

Louden, W. (1992). Understanding reflection through collaborative research. In A. Hargreaves & M. Fullan (Eds.), *Understanding teacher development* (pp. 178-215). London: Cassell.

Madaus, G., West, M. M., Harmon, M. C., Lomax, R. G., Viator, K. A., Mungal, C. F., Butler, P. A., McDowell, C., Simmons, R., & Sweeney, E. (1992). *The influence of* testing on teaching math and science in grades 4-12. Boston: Boston College, Center for the Study of Testing, Evaluation, and Educational Policy.

Maglathlin, H. B. (1866). *Greenleaf's new practical arithmetic*. Cambridge, MA: H. O. Houghton.

McLaughlin, M. B., & Yee, S. M. (1988). School as a place to have a career. In A. Lieberman (Ed.), *Building a professional culture in schools* (pp. 23-44). New York: Teachers College Press.

McNeil, L. M., & McNeil, M. S. (1994). When good theory makes bad practice. *Theory Into Practice, 33*(4), 254-260.

McNight, C. C., Grosswith, F. J., Dossey, J. A., Kifer, E., Swafford, J. O., Trevers, K. J., & Cooney, T. J. (1987). *The underachieving curriculum: Assessing U.S. school mathematics from an international perspective*. Champaign, IL: Stipes.

Miles, M. (1983). Unraveling the mystery of institutionalization. *Educational Leadership, 41*(3), 14-27.

Mirel, J. (1994). School reform unplugged: The Bensenville new American school project, 1991-1993. *American Educational Research Journal, 35*(3), 481-518.

National Council of Teachers of Mathematics, Commission on Standards for School Mathematics. (1989a). *New directions for elementary school mathematics: 1989 yearbook*. Reston, VA: Author.

National Council of Teachers of Mathematics, Commission on Standards for School Mathematics. (1989b). *Curriculum and evaluation standards for school mathematics*. Reston, VA: Author.

National Education Commission on Time and Learning. (1994). *Prisoners of time*. Washington, DC: Government Printing Office.

Nesher, P. (1988). Multiplicative school word problems: Theoretical approaches and empirical findings. In J. Hiebert & M. Behr (Eds.), *Number concepts and operations in the middle grades* (pp. 19-40). Reston, VA: Lawrence Erlbaum and National Council of Teachers of Mathematics.

Ogawa, R. T. (1994). The institutional sources of educational reform: The case of school-based management. *American Educational Research Journal, 35*(3), 519-548.

Parris, C. (1993). *Teacher agency and curriculum-making in classrooms*. New York: Teachers College Press.

Patterson, J. L., Purkey, S., & Parker, J. V. (1986). *Productive school systems for a non-rational world*. Alexandria, VA: Association for Supervision and Curriculum Development.

Peterson, P., & Fennema, E. (1985). Effective teaching, student engagement in classroom activities, and sex related differences in learning mathematics. *American Educational Research Journal, 18*, 453-473.

Piaget, J. (1977). *The development of thought: Equilibration of cognitive structures*. New York: Viking.

Polya, G. (1981). *Mathematical discovery*. New York: John Wiley.

Porter, A., Floden, R., Freeman, D., Schmidt, W., & Schwille, J. (1988). Content determinants in elementary school mathematics. In D. Grouws, T. V. Cooney, & P. Jones (Eds.), *Effective mathematics teaching* (pp. 96-110). Reston, VA: National Council of Teachers of Mathematics.

Reitzug, U. C. (1994). A case study of empowering principal behavior. *American Educational Research Journal, 31*(2), 283-307.

Resnick, L. B. (1983). A developmental theory of number understanding. In H. Ginsburg (Ed.), *The development of mathematical thinking* (pp. 110-149). New York: Academic Press.

Resnick, L. B. (1992, Spring). Why we need national standards and exams. *State Education Leader*, 4-5. (Quarterly publication available from the ECS Distribution Center, Denver, CO)

# References

Resnick, L. B., & Resnick, D. (1989). Tests as standards of achievement in schools. *The uses of standardized tests in American education.* Princeton, NJ: Educational Testing Service.

Reyes, P. (1990). Individual work orientation and teacher outcomes. *Journal of Educational Research, 86,* 327-334.

Rutter, M., Maughan, B., Mortimer, P., Ouston, J., & Smith, A. (1979). *Fifteen thousand hours: Secondary schools and their effects on children.* Cambridge, MA: Harvard University Press.

Sarason, S. B. (1972) *The creation of settings and the future societies.* San Francisco: Jossey-Bass.

Sarason, S. B. (1983). *Schooling in America.* New York: Free Press.

Sarason, S. B. (1990). *The predictable failure of educational reform.* San Francisco: Jossey-Bass.

Sarason, S. B. (1993). *The case for change.* San Francisco: Jossey-Bass.

Schön, D. (1983). *The reflective practitioner: How professionals think in action.* New York: Basic Books.

Schön, D. (1987). *Educating the reflective practitioner.* San Francisco: Jossey-Bass.

Sergiovanni, T. J. (1990). Adding value to leadership gets extraordinary results. *Educational Leadership, 47*(8), 23-27.

Sharan, S., Kussell, P., Hertz-Lazarowitz, R., Bejarano, Y., Raviv, S., & Sharan, Y. (1984). *Cooperative learning in the classroom: Research in segregated schools.* Hillsdale, NJ: Lawrence Erlbaum.

Sizer, T. (1984). *Horace's compromise: The dilemma of the American high school.* Boston: Houghton Mifflin.

Slavin, R. (1983). *Cooperative learning.* New York: Longman.

Smith, L., Prunty, J., Dwyer, D. C., & Kleine, P. F. (1986). Reconstructing educational innovation. In A. Lieberman (Ed.), *Rethinking school improvement* (pp. 82-95). New York: Teachers College Press.

Solomon, P. G. (1977). *An investigation of the problems of moving school controlled high school education from classroom to community.* Unpublished doctoral dissertation, Columbia University, New York.

Solomon, P. G. (1994, April). *Team teaching in the Saturday Morning Search for Solutions program.* Paper presented at the annual meeting of the American Educational Research Association, Atlanta, GA. (ERIC Document Reproduction Service No. ED 370 935)

Solomon, P. G. (1995, April). *The elements of peer interaction in an effective delivery of constructivist inservice education.* Paper presented at the annual meeting of the American Educational Research Association, San Francisco.

Sowder, J. T. (1988). Mental computation and number comparison: Their roles in the development of number sense and computational estimation. In J. Hiebert & M. Behr (Eds.), *Number concepts and operations in the middle grades* (pp. 182-197). Reston, VA: Lawrence Erlbaum and National Council of Teachers of Mathematics.

Sowder, J. T. (1992). Making sense of numbers. In G. Leinhardt (Ed.), *Analysis of arithmetic for mathematics teaching* (pp. 1-51). Hillsdale, NJ: Lawrence Erlbaum.

Spady, W., & Marshall, K. (1990, June). *Vail leadership seminars.* Unpublished material from seminar at Bear Mountain, NY.

Steen, L. A. (1989). Teaching mathematics for tomorrow's world. *Educational Leadership, 47*(1), 18-22.

Stenhouse, L. (1985). *Research as a basis for teaching: Readings from the works of Lawrence Stenhouse* (J. Rudduck & D. Hopkins, Eds.). London: Heinemann.

Stevenson, H. W. (1987). America's math problems. *Educational Leadership, 45*(2), 4-10.

Stevenson, H. W. (1988). *The polished stones* [Videotape]. Ann Arbor: University of Michigan, Board of Regents.

Tannen, D. (1994, August 28). How to give orders to a man. *New York Times Magazine*, p. 46.
Theobold, R. (1987). *The rapids of change: Social entrepreneurship for turbulent times.* Indianapolis, IN: Knowledge Systems.
Thoreau, H. D. (1893). *A week on the Concord and Merrimack Rivers.* Boston: Houghton Mifflin. (Original work published 1849)
Tyack, D., & Tobin, W. (1994). The "grammar" of schooling: Why has it been so hard to change? *American Educational Research Journal, 31*(3), 453-478.
Tyson-Bernstein, H. (1988). The academy's contribution to the impoverishment of America's textbooks. *Phi Delta Kappan, 69*, 193-198.
University of the State of New York: The State Education Department. (1984). *Regents action plan to improve elementary and secondary education results in New York State.* Albany: Author.
University of the State of New York: The State Education Department. (1990). *Time management: Managing instructional time to enhance program congruence.* Albany: Author.
University of the State of New York: The State Education Department. (1991). *The new compact for learning.* Albany: Author.
University of the State of New York: The State Education Department. (1994). *Learning centered curriculum and assessment for New York State.* Albany: Author.
U.S. Department of Education. (1990). *America 2000: An education strategy.* Washington, DC: Author.
Van Lehn, K. (1986). Arithmetic procedures are induced from examples. In J. Hiebert (Ed.), *Conceptual and procedural knowledge: The case of mathematics* (pp. 133-179). Hillsdale, NJ: Lawrence Erlbaum.
Vygotsky, L. S. (1978). Educational implications: Interactions between learning and development (M. Lopez-Morillas, Trans.). In M. Cole, V. J. Steiner, S. Scriber, & E. Sauberman (Eds.), *Mind in society: The development of higher psychological processes* (pp. 79-91). Cambridge, MA: Harvard University Press.
von Glasersfeld, E. (1990). Environment and communication. In L. P. Steffe & T. Wood (Eds.), *Transforming children's mathematics education: International perspectives* (pp. 30-38). Hillsdale, NJ: Lawrence Erlbaum.
Weick, K. E. (1976). Educational organizations as loosely coupled systems. *Administrative Science Quarterly, 21*(1), 1-19.
Weiss, C. H. (1993). Shared decision making about what? *Teachers College Record, 95*(1), 69-92.
Westervelt, E. D. (1993). *Parents as decision makers: Perceptions of role and involvement.* Unpublished doctoral dissertation, Fordham University, New York.
Wiggins, G. (1989a). Teaching to the authentic test. *Educational Leadership, 46*(7), 41-47.
Wiggins, G. (1989b). A true test: Toward more equitable assessment. *Phi Delta Kappan, 70*, 703-708.
Wilford, J. N. (1994, November 1). Big bangs defenders weigh fudge factor, a blunder of Einstein's, as a fix for new crisis. *New York Times*, p. C1.
Wise, A. E., & Darling-Hammond, L. (1984). Teacher evaluation and teacher professionalism. *Educational Leadership, 41*(4), 28-33.
Wood, T., & Cobb, P. (1990). The contextual nature of teaching: Mathematics and reading instruction in one second grade classroom. *The Elementary School Journal, 90*, 499-502.
Zakariya, S. B. (1983). *Effective instructional management.* Arlington, VA: American Association of School Administrators.

# Index

Absorption learning, 119
Accountability, 29, 31, 71, 74, 84, 97, 114, 153
   peer review, 115
   personal by teachers, 157
Action path of change, 12, 106
Administrators:
   training, 80
Alan, 60-61, 85
American Association for the Advancement of Science, 145, 167
Anderson, J. R., 82, 133, 167
Anne, 64-66
Argyris, C., 58
Assessment, 85, 135-159
   articulation with curriculum, 136-137
   discontinuities with curriculum (Figure 7.1), 139
   math assessment in South Vale, 154
   publishing and disseminating results, 148
   reflective practice, 10
   reviewing results, 154
   reviewing results and redesigning, 148
Assimilation:
   template for, 147

Back to basics, 22
Baroody, A. J., 133, 153
Barr, R., 51, 69
Bartering, building, and bonding, 26
Barth, R., 99, 114
Bell, C. H., 97, 105
Bennett, B., 9, 108, 158
Bennett, C. R., 108, 136, 158
Bennis, W., 17, 58, 59, 74
Berger, R., 10
Blakeslee, S., 181
Board of Education:
   power, 100
   reports, 98
Brandt, R., 167
Building and district leadership teams:
   hiring new staff, 114
Building leadership teams. *See also* Site-based teams

BLT formation, 44
  curriculum, 115
  new capacities and
    accomplishments, 111
  ownership, 111
  teachers' feelings, 112
Burnout, 7, 175
  cause, 113
Burns, R., 177

California Achievement Tests, 47, 90, 103, 125, 141, 155, 159, 168
Capacity, 57, 59, 77, 96, 97, 105-134, 137
  assimilation stage, 147-149
  building, 87-88, 99, 163, 168
  competency level, 157-158
  defined, 7, 14, 132
  energy requirement, 106
  growth-a metaphor, 117
  interacting variables, 74, 106
  leader support for, 102, 103, 178
  need for, 171, 175
  overcoming resistance, 106
  required energy, 113
  teacher growth, 37, 39, 61, 68, 173
  template for growth in, 116-117
  time for growth, 168
  to manage collaboratively, 110
Carnegie Commission, 22
Carpenter, T. P., 149
Change, 1-179
  chronology, 95
  force for, 75
  history of success, 83
  honeymoon period, 36
  lack of clarity and consistency, 99
  preparation for, 91
  requirements, 23
  teacher behavior, 96
  teacher involvement, 95
  variables of change, 12, 13 (Figure 1.1)
Changing people, 105-133
Classroom observations, 71

Cobb, P., 132, 149
Cogan, M., 128
Cognition:
  conceptual and procedural knowledge, 149
Cole, M., 32
Collegial clusters, 71, 89, 99, 121-125, 174, 177, 179
  different forms of, 164-165
  elementary math planning, 66-68
  high school department strength, 73
  value of integrated and protean groups, 7, 48-50, 64, 165
Connecting curriculum and school improvement, 8-10, 103, 136-137, 158
Consensual domain, 12, 123, 128, 132, 149, 150
Constructivism, 36, 125, 128, 133
  current emphasis, 118
  defined, 23, 132
  teachers construct new knowledge, 131, 132
Consultants:
  use of, 122-123
Cooper, M., 111
Cooperative learning, 2, 16, 23, 108, 112, 120, 124
Cox, P., 94
Crandall, D. P., 94
Curriculum, 135-159
  activities, 146
  agreeing on measures, 148, 153
  consensual mastery, 139
  consensus, 146
  content standards and measures, 148
  discontinuities in design (Figure 7.1), 139
  documents, 146
  generation, 146
  listening to parents' voices, 146
  making choices, 148, 150
  needing documentation, 148
  objectives, 146
  ownership, 152

# Index

present state, 138
scope and sequence, 152-154
sharing with parents, 155
role of expert, 150
stakeholders' words, 148, 150
teacher autonomy, 150
teachers as writers, 146

Darling-Hammond, L., 71, 97, 158
Deal, T. E., 34
Deanna, 82-83
Decision making:
 difficulty of change, 98
 *See also* Shared decison making
Decision-making terminals, 91, 95, 97
Defensive focusing, 90
Departmental clusters, 73
Diene's blocks, 133
Differences in perception or
 perspective, 28, 30-31
 national, 30
 South Vale, 30
DiNatale, J., 179
District leadership team:
 formation, 28, 43
Documentation:
 in reaching ownership, 137
Documenting curriculum and
 assessment:
 template for, 148
Donohue, T., 162, 163, 165, 174
Double-bind messages, 39, 84
Dossey, J. A., 32, 56

Edmonds, R. R., 32
Effective schools, 27, 32
 criteria, 44
Elaine, 11, 66-68, 119, 176
Energy expenditures for change
 (Figure 8.1), 172
English, F. W., 138
Entropy, 57, 174
Equity, 84-86, 136-140, 168
Evidence of "bonding," 26

Evocator, 79, 109, 123, 132
 defined, 17
 power, 129
 support, 102
Expectations, 84-86
 transfer, 82

Facilitation, 126-127
Facilitation and possibility, 78
Fennema, E., 56
Finn, C. E., Jr., 30
Firestone, W. A., 64
Formative evaluation, 88, 89
 difference between the
  experimental and control
  teacher group, 103
 questionnaire, 89
 tests, 90
French, W. L., 97, 105
Fullan, M., 6, 9, 10, 75, 107, 136, 137, 168, 177
Funding:
 budgeting for additional paid
  preparation time, 164
 evocator control, 102
 local (hard) money, 103
 soft money, 101
Fuson, K. C., 159

Gay, J., 32
Gary, 37, 48
Ginsburg, H. P., 32
Glasser, W., 82
Glatthorn, A. A., 51, 107, 139
Goals for 2000, 145
Goodson, I. F., 17, 107
Governance, 4, 7, 8, 18, 40, 74, 103, 107, 159, 164, 171, 174, 177, 178. *See also* Site-based collaborative decision making
Greta, 36, 68, 91, 92, 106

Hansen, K. H., 79
Herrick, R., 161

History, 12, 13, 15, 33-55, 179
　agrarian, 1
　curriculum, 138, 152
　of change, 55, 83, 158, 177
　personal, 136
　role of, 33, 117, 123, 125
　South Vale, 5, 38-42, 63, 64, 66, 80, 82, 143, 178
　template for documenting history and setting, 42-43
　variable of, 12, 13, 15, 93, 106, 158
Hopkins, 96, 107, 158
Huberman, M., 14, 78, 82, 90

Inconsistency of leadership, 29
Indirect messages, 18
Informal culture, 97, 105
Intangible resources, 117
　time, 124

Jean Brown, 38, 166
Jill, 85
Jim, 5, 61-64, 110
Johnson, D. W., 16, 108
Johnson, R. T., 16, 108
Johnson-Holubec, E., 16, 108
Joyce, B. R., 107, 108, 109, 117, 158

Kerman, S., 63, 115
Kilpatrick, J., 35

Lave, J., 32
Leadership, 57-103
　commitment, 72
　consistency, 39-41, 54, 61, 72, 106, 144
　dealing with history, 3, 55, 159
　defined, 12-15, 57-58
　effective schools, 28
　energy, 170-171
　failure, 39
　gaining power by giving, 66
　lack of support by, 98, 110, 111, 173

　new leaders, 61
　patterns, 3, 61, 64, 66, 68, 74, 102, 139
　power management, 102
　sources, 7, 60, 74-75
　sources of power, 60, 63, 165
　support and pressure by, 48, 75-103, 117, 171
　time, 163, 170
　trust of, 125
　*See also* Power; Teacher leadership
Lecture With Practice, 121
Less is more, 167
Lieberman, A., 30, 79, 112
Lila, 128, 176
Linde, C., 18
Linking classroom and school improvement, 136
Little, J. W., 107, 115
Longstreet, W. S., 138
Lortie, D. C., 2, 36, 69, 91, 131, 157
Louden, W., 108

Madaus, G., 142
Maglathlin, H. B., 35
Manipulatives, 119
　as abstractions, 133
　history of use, 52
　needed transitions, 125
　use of, 127
Marshall, K., 14, 94
Mathematics, 1-179
　existing program, 46
　high school department, 81
　practical value, 53
McNeil, 136, 165
McNight, C. C., 32, 52
Meg, 62, 94-95
Mentors, 176. *See also* Peer coaching
Middle school:
　philosophical differences, 25
　priorities, 45
Miles, M., 14, 78, 94, 112
Miller, L., 30, 79
Mirel, J., 6

# Index

Modeling, 117, 127, 129, 130
Monitoring, 126, 127
Monitoring and feedback, 128

Nanus, B., 17, 58, 59, 74
National Assessment of Educational Progress, 56
National Council of Teachers of Mathematics:
  standards, 89, 95, 119, 122, 125, 145
  vision of, 23
  yearbook, 91
Needs assessment:
  analysis of data, 51
  open-ended, 43
  template, 42-43
Needs assessment committee:
  formation, 48
Nesher, P., 159
New Compact for Learning, 3, 142

Objectives:
  discrepancy between written and taught, 51
  *See also* Outcomes
Ogawa, R. T., 18
Outcomes, 131
  agreement on, 50
  alignment, 89
  attention to, 110, 118
  conceptual, 154
  connections to improvement activities, 110
  consensus, 14, 89
  contracts, 137
  focus on, 29
  implementation dip, 168
  importance, 5
  improvement, 7
  in your own words, 153
  matching, 152
  outcome-based education, 4
  paradigm shift, 30
  peer review of, 158
  procedural, 150
  responsibility, 159
  setting direction for, 177
  standards, 4
  tests, 99, 143
  writing, 146
Ownership, 23, 36, 135-159
  assimilation stage, 118, 137
  belonging to the team, 111
  capacity, 14, 106, 132
  disclaiming, 152
  documentation, 137
  growth, 154
  impediments, 12
  new practice, 105
  new program, 123
  of new knowledge, 132
  power, 70
  previous comfort, 55
  rigors of change, 23
  time, 15
  timetables, 173
  transfer, 4
  voice and vision, 23
  volunteers, 87

Paradox of prodding, 79
Parents:
  capacity, 106, 113, 122, 136, 146, 148, 155-157
  Chinese and Japanese attribution for success, 52
  concerns, 1, 2, 22, 36, 38, 69, 73, 141, 143, 155
  involvement, 5, 8, 11, 15, 23, 24, 28, 30, 50, 51, 74, 89, 148, 159, 166
  power, 58-60
  principal relationships, 97
  standards, 141
  teacher relationships, 42, 49, 71, 92, 99, 110
  time for participation, 166, 168
  values, 38, 42, 47, 52, 53, 55, 68, 69, 84, 85, 131, 157
  vision sharing, 147, 155
  vision transfer, 105, 106

voices, 19, 60, 146, 166
Parker, J. V., 23, 48
Park Lane, 96, 174-176
   yearly plan, 170
Parris, C., 150
Part/whole relationships, 132, 149
Patterson, J. L., 23, 48
Peer coaching, 5, 63, 107, 117, 126-128, 130
   apprentice/expert relationship, 109
   coaching and feedback, 128
   elements, 130
Peer interactions, 133
Peer observation, 116
Peer reflections, 10-12, 107-110, 118-119, 148, 154
   time and energy, 116
   *See also* Reflective practice
Pennell, J. K., 64
Performance of students:
   as verification for teachers, 90
Personal visions, 19
Peter, 29, 44, 61
Peterson, P., 56
Philosophy:
   sharing, 95
Piaget, J., 36, 118, 133
Piloting teachers, 90, 95, 96, 120, 121, 124
   formative evaluation, 88
   microculture, 87
   teaching assistants, 72
Planning clusters, 66
Polya, G., 36
Porter, A., 69
Posner, J., 32
Possibility, 127
   a form of support, 121
Power, 57-103
   as currency, 74
   cultural norms, 87
   defined, 11-15, 58
   exercising control, 122
   from success, 83
   giving and using, 57, 59 (Figure 4.1), 61, 63, 66-73, 99
   giving messages, 18-19
   government, 84
   history, 63
   holding on, 7, 99
   in pressure and support, 80
   in the classroom, 70-71
   of principals, 5, 29, 63, 71, 72
   of teachers, 1, 9, 15, 31, 68-70
   of tests, 90
   other power sources, 60, 72-74
   patterns in South Vale, 40, 44, 64-66, 68
   possession, 14
   preserves, 3, 31, 53, 55, 60, 68
   tangible resource, money as, 101
   tension over, 80
   transfer of power, 19, 59 (Figure 4.1)
   variable of change, 11-15
Practice, 117, 123
Preparation for program reform:
   mathematics, 54
Pressure, 77-103
   actions, 79 (Figure 5.1), 102
   defined, 12, 14, 77-78, 102
   from colleagues, 71, 129
   from parents and community, 53, 63, 73, 100
   internal and external, 99
   needing, 11, 87-88, 106
   of new roles, 97
   of state mandates, 99
   of time, 171
   overcoming, 15, 103
   political, 139
   power components, 77, 78, 80
   to participate in SBCDM, 98, 103
   with support, 79, 80, 93, 94-97
   *See also* Power; Support
Principals:
   consistency, 62
   developing leaders, 64
   district leadership team, 28, 29
   energies, 62
   expected to give away power, 98
   involvement in math needs assessment, 48

# Index

new, 29
power, 59, 60, 62, 63, 70, 72
receptivity to change, 55
reluctance to give
    decision-making power, 97
resistance to site-based
    management, 5
roles, 25, 55
sharing power, 114
site-based management, 27
support, 72
time, 62, 72
Problem solving, 22, 122, 128
Professional development, 106
    defined, 107
    inservice, 126
    Japan, 163
    planning, 116
    reflective practice, 109
    South Vale workshops, 126
    student performance, 168
    teacher as researcher, 108
    template for building capacity, 117
    *See also* Capacity
Purkey, S., 23, 48

Reasoning skills, 119
Reculturization, 136, 137, 145, 155
    template for, 147
    when it occurred, 157
Reflective planning, 117, 118
Reflective practice:
    functional level of change, 10-12
    in action, 135
    on action in peer reflections, 135
    on action; in action, 109
    peer interactions, 132
    structured interaction, 125
    transformation, 109
Regents, 85
    classes, 169
    curriculum, 53
    exam, 47
Reitzug, U. C., 58, 78, 101, 127
Research, 127

Resistance:
    overcoming, 91-97, 131-133
    understanding, 91-93
Resnick, D., 140
Resnick, L. B., 122, 133, 140, 159
Responsibility:
    after collegial decision making, 96
    opportunities for peer observation, 116
    sharing responsibility and power, 71
Restructuring, 136
Reyes, P., 157
Roles:
    changing, 97
    group norms, 97
Russell, R., 32
Rutter, M., 32

Sandy, 112-114, 163
Sarason, S. B., 2, 6, 9, 10, 33, 55, 70, 80, 95, 136, 164, 170, 171
Saxl, E. R., 112
Schedule:
    constraints of, 99
    power, 86
    power of high school, 73
Scholastic Aptitude Tests (S.A.T.), 21, 47, 51, 53
Schön, D., 10
School reform and restructuring:
    interaction between governance and curriculum change, 103
    national vision origins, 18
Science Curriculum Improvement Study (SCIS), 159
2061—Science for All Americans, 145
Scope and sequence, 152-154
Sergiovanni, T. J., 24
Setting goals, 118
    focus, 119
Shane, H. G., 138
Sharan, S., 16
Shared decision making, 3, 92, 136, 177

as a cultural obligation, 164
as a professional obligation, 164
as organizational change, 136
confusion, 9
connected to program change, 9
history, 19
in New York and Florida, 9
inconsistent vision, 30
limiting, 165
overall climate, 10
South Vale beginnings, 27
state mandate, 98
*See also* Decision making;
  Site-based collaborative
  decision making
Showers, B., 107, 109, 117
Site-based collaborative decision
  making (SBCDM), 34, 44
  autonomy, 7
  building teacher leaders, 60
  congruency in vision, 100
  funding, 101, 103
  growth of capacity, 116
  high school, 72-74
  leadership, 80, 99
  leadership support, 173
  mandate, 177
  power and control, 87
  preparation, 54
  problem solving, 113
  time, 163
  vision, 64
  voices, 91
Site-based teams (BLTs), 5, 36, 43,
  48, 49, 60-63, 65, 81, 85, 91,
  99-101, 103, 110-112, 115, 159,
  164, 165, 169, 174, 175, 177
  BLT-high school, 73
  BLT-leaders, 98
  BLT-Park Lane, 66, 170
  documenting success, 6
  gaining capacity, 110
  need for new skills, 110
  ownership, 86
  priorities, 5
Sizer, T., 167
Slavin, R., 16, 23

Smith, L., 34
Socioeconomic disaggregation of
  test scores, 29, 32
Solomon, P. G., 158, 164
South Vale:
  achievements, 6
  description of setting, 39-41
  organization, 46
  performance on tests, 47
  history of SBCDM, 5
Sowder, J. T., 23
Spady, W., 14, 94
Staff development. *See also*
  Professional development
  defined, 107
  traditional, 116, 121
  traditional in-service, 121
Stakeholders:
  parents, 157
  shared visions, 145
Standards:
  equity with common standards,
    141
  setting, 50
  setting by teachers, 71
  shared vision, 145
  transition from objectives, 152
  *See also* Outcomes
State (State Education
    Department), 163
  change, 177
  collegial clusters, 165
  compact for learning, 145
  curriculum, 47, 51, 53, 142, 145,
    146, 149-152, 159
  effective schools, 44
  funds, 101, 103
  mandate, 3, 4, 29, 39
  mandates, 3, 73, 84, 92, 98, 99,
    177
  power, 60
  reporting, 142
  standards, 150
  testing, 143
  tests, 47, 83, 90, 92, 135, 151
  time, 167
Steen, L. A., 86

# Index

Steffy, B. E., 138
Stenhouse, L., 108
Stevenson, H. W., 163
Students:
  confidence, 52
  control, 124
  control of, 127
  expectations, 52
  giving power to, 82
  listening to verbalizations, 152
  power, 61
  problems of individuals, 127
Support, 77-103, 127, 142
  actions, 79 (Figure 5.1), 102
  collegial, 11, 123
  defined, 12-14, 77-78, 102
  for curriculum writing, 153
  for SBCDM, 63, 98-101, 110
  for new teacher capacity,
    124-131, 153, 168
  for the past history of change, 15
  from evocators, 102, 171
  from parents, 24, 157
  from and for principals, 65, 72,
    114
  from teacher leaders, 68
  from teachers' union, 28
  giving power as, 80, 84-87
  needing, 94-101, 110
  pressure balance, 93, 94
  tangible resources, 100-101,
    119-121
  time, 124
  *See also* Power; Pressure
Supported enforcement/
  assistance, 14, 78


Tangible resources, 100-101, 117,
  119
Tannen, D., 18
Teacher leaders, 7, 66, 68, 73, 111,
  176
  accepting responsibility, 174
  energy resources, 136
  implementation dip, 176
  power, 86

stress, 98
*See also* Alan; Elaine; Sandy
Teachers:
  as evocators, 130
  as researchers, 108, 123, 125
  attitudes, 36, 37
  capacity for developing math
    concepts, 151
  control of timetables, 93, 174
  empowering, 9, 119
  energies, 93
  individual autonomy, 137, 139
  influencing others, 97
  lack of history in new
    approaches, 125
  overloads, 37
  rewards, 92
  shifting blame, 37, 49
  teacher-evaluation, 128
  teaming, 164
  time, 92
Teachers' union, 5, 28, 81
  time and teaching day, 164
Teaching assistants, 90, 127
  BLT, 43
  needed in SBCDM, 164
  piloting teachers, 72
Tests:
  as controls, 141
  as prodders or impediments for
    change, 143
  authentic, 140
  controlling curriculum, 142
  in minority schools, 142
  in South Vale, 143
  power of, 140
Texts 120, 125
  as determiners of curriculum,
    144
  presure to cover, 144
  power of, 143-145
  school cultures, 145
Theobold, R., 22
Thoreau, H. D., 179
Time, 161-179
  as an intangible resource, 79,
    102, 124

as a variable of change, 162
compensation for, 48, 66, 163
competition for, 10, 64, 69, 73, 92, 93, 117, 122
defined, 15
for collaborative planning and decision-making, 7, 43, 48, 62, 64, 153, 162-164
for curriculum writing, 147-148, 153
for instruction, 46, 49, 51-53, 56, 61, 69, 83, 84, 86, 90, 103, 106, 119, 123-124, 166-168
for leader or evocator support, 127
for passage, 6, 7, 10, 88-89, 113, 161, 168, 171
for peer observations, 116
for professional growth, 117, 123, 127, 132, 163
for listening to history, voices and building trust, 24, 36, 43, 52-53, 91
in neuro-science, 181
in preparation for tests, 142
in school day and calendar, 162
provided in other countries, 167
priorities, 127
regression through passage, 40, 106, 174
resource, 162
serendipity or timeliness, 32, 35, 39, 80, 85, 105, 176-177
spent by parents, 157, 166
the implementation dip, 168
three perspectives of, 162
Timetables, 170
control over, 93, 102, 170, 173
decision making, 90, 95
overloaded, 91
Tobin, W., 177
Tom, 24
Top-down support for bottom-up reform, 142
Tracking, 85, 169
Trust:
among colleagues, 74
peer review, 116

Tyack, D., 177

United States Department of Education, 145
University of the State of New York, 145, 163

Van Lehn, K., 56
Variables of change:
definitions, 12-14
Visions, 17-32
and power, 77
changes in math, 34
conflict in, 32, 61-63, 75, 95, 98, 100, 102, 123
defined, 12, 17
differences in perception, 29-32, 114, 165, 173
global, 18, 21-22
in context, 21-22
national source of (for school reform), 18-19
personal source of (for math), 19-21
personal source of (for shared decision making), 24-27
sources of, 40, 54, 85, 178
systemic source of (for school improvement), 27-30
transfer of and ownership of, 18-30, 40, 42, 44, 50, 54, 105, 132, 146
Vocabulary for discourse, 128
Voices, 12, 15, 17-32, 50, 54
congruence, 165
defined, 18
indirect, 18
history and setting, 36, 37, 42-43
listening to, 1, 24, 40, 54, 56, 63, 64, 81, 91, 95, 97, 106, 117, 146, 148, 176, 177, 178
parent, 1, 39, 66
von Glasersfeld, E., 23, 82, 118, 132
Vygotsky, L. S., 119

# Index

Wandering around, 127
Weiss, C. H., 10
Westervelt, E., 56, 159, 166
Weick, K. E., 31, 57
Wiggins, G., 140
Wilford, J. N., 161
Wise, A. E., 71
Wood, T., 149

Yee, S. M., 102
Young untenured teachers, 175

Zakariya, S. B., 48
Zalesnick, A., 58

**The Corwin Press logo**—a raven striding across an open book—represents the happy union of courage and learning. We are a professional-level publisher of books and journals for K-12 educators, and we are committed to creating and providing resources that embody these qualities. Corwin's motto is "Success for All Learners."